"While the schema therapy library is rich with books for clinicians, there are few available for individuals struggling to understand the impact of schemas and modes in their daily lives. Richard Brouillette has created a wonderful meditative tool and workbook, perfect for those individuals on a path of self-discovery as well as those working in tandem with a therapist."

—**Peregrine M. Kavros, PhD, MBA, MDiv**, chair of the ISST Ethics & Conflict Resolution Committee, director of Schema Therapy Institute SouthEast, and advanced schema therapist supervisor/trainer

"In 1994, Jeffrey Young and Janet Klosko's book, *Reinventing Your Life*, was a pathbreaking and profound handbook on how schemas intrude on and distort our daily lives. Now, Richard Brouillette offers an exciting successor, a timely update mirroring new development, including mindfulness, as well as an energizing journaling. Richard helps you move from feeling like a bystander to becoming the director in the 'theater of your life.' This is a brilliant and extremely practical book!"

—**Eckhard Roediger, MD**, director of the Frankfurt Schema Therapy Institute, past president of the International Society of Schema Therapy (ISST), and coauthor of *Contextual Schema Therapy*

"Richard Brouillette has written an innovative, dialogue-centered book on schema therapy. Emphasizing the core importance of our internal self-talk, he teaches us how to use chairwork, imagery rescripting, and writing as ways to compassionately engage with and effectively heal our inner pain and suffering. This book will be a gift not only for those seeking to change their lives, but also for clinicians looking for more profound methods of healing."

—**Scott Kellogg, PhD**, director of the Transformational Chairwork Psychotherapy Project, and author of *Transformational Chairwork*

"Ever wondered why we repeat the same coping patterns, even when they prevent us from reaching our potential? Even with great commitment and self-determination, we often find ourselves stuck in entrenched and habitual ways of managing our lives. In this book, your inner life will be revealed through powerful techniques that uproot old self-sabotaging coping patterns, paving the way for self-insight and healthier ways of coping. Written by one of the luminaries of the schema therapy field. Read and be inspired."

—**Susan Simpson, ClinPsyD**, director of Schema Therapy Scotland, and coauthor/editor of *Schema Therapy for Eating Disorders*

"I cannot recommend *Your Coping Skills Aren't Working* highly enough. Richard Brouilette has written a smart and accessible book on how to change unhealthy patterns related to interpersonal conflicts and other life challenges that is psychologically sophisticated while still being clear, concise, and user-friendly. It reads like having a friend next to you guiding you through a process toward healthier ways of being."

—**Jeff Conway, MS, LCSW**, president of the ISST, and founding member of the ISST and The NY Center for Emotion Focused Therapy

"Adults often ignore the child within; yet learning to embrace this part can create profound insight and happiness. Developing a positive connection between our adult self and the younger version is the healing intention of this wonderful book. Powerful therapeutic strategies are woven into a compelling, user-friendly format for personal growth. This book resonated deeply with my inner child—let it do the same for yours."

—**Kathryn Rudlin, LCSW**, advanced certified schema therapist, supervisor, trainer, and director at California Schema Therapy Training Program; and author of *Ghost Mothers*

"This is a practical, easy-to-follow book that will assist readers to understand their unhelpful coping patterns and learn better ways of meeting their emotional needs. The examples provided are excellent and easy to implement on a day-to-day basis. I think this book will resonate with anyone who wants to improve their mental health and well-being. I highly recommend this book."

—**Tena Davies, MaClin Psych**, clinical psychologist, and advanced certified schema therapist

Your coping skills aren't working.

HOW TO **BREAK FREE** FROM THE HABITS THAT ONCE HELPED YOU BUT NOW HOLD YOU BACK

RICHARD BROUILLETTE, LCSW

New Harbinger Publications, Inc.

Publisher's Note

This publication is designed to provide accurate and authoritative information in regard to the subject matter covered. It is sold with the understanding that the publisher is not engaged in rendering psychological, financial, legal, or other professional services. If expert assistance or counseling is needed, the services of a competent professional should be sought.

NEW HARBINGER PUBLICATIONS is a registered trademark of New Harbinger Publications, Inc.

New Harbinger Publications is an employee-owned company.

Cover design by Sara Christian

Acquired by Jennye Garibaldi

Edited by Gretel Hakanson

Library of Congress Cataloging-in-Publication Data on file

Printed in the United States of America

25   24   23

10   9   8   7   6   5   4   3   2   1   First Printing

To my wife, Cathy.

"If music be the food of love, play on!"

Contents

Foreword

People often come to psychotherapists in distress regarding a feeling of being flawed or defective, lonely, isolated, or deprived that is often accompanied by a self-defeating pattern that is making their life hard...a behavior, feeling, or thought that is difficult to change. *"I just can't stop doing it, and I don't know why"* is a common plea.

Whether it's dealing with the feeling of walking around like an imposter in your own skin, unable to share your feelings with others or advocate for yourself, or struggling to manage your angry outbursts, the fact is, all humans face certain challenges in daily life and longstanding patterns that may be linked with personal life narratives. These unchallenged "truths" about who we are and how the world works may cause us to get stuck on the journey to change, making it difficult to get out of our own way.

Long-standing coping styles, while helpful when we are small and powerless, may not be easily unlearned as we launch into adulthood. These coping styles can become self-defeating over time and may perpetuate the very consequences we seek to avoid. In other words, your coping skills are part of the problem, triggering the all-too-familiar and upsetting outcomes. The therapist facilitates a process where clients learn to observe activating conditions that lead to implicitly memorized behavioral responses and reimagine (through integrated strategies) a corrective emotional experience—one in which they get their early unmet emotional needs met. It's a challenging endeavor—bypassing lifelong ways of coping and sustaining distance from deeply imbedded beliefs. And, once accomplished, the work is about developing healthy patterns for living in the world and effectively relating with others.

In 1993, Jeffrey Young and Janet Klosko wrote *Reinventing Your Life* as a self-help book that translated Jeffrey Young's schema therapy model for the general reader audience. They introduced the term "lifetrap" as a way of understanding long-held biased emotional beliefs that get triggered under certain reminiscent conditions, deepening the grooves of distress and dissatisfaction.

As an expert in schema therapy and founder and director of the Cognitive Therapy Center of New Jersey and The Schema Therapy Institutes of New Jersey, New York City, and Washington, DC, I have decades of experience witnessing the relief the schema therapy approach offers to people with maladaptive coping reactions, or lifetraps. I have a specialty in working with individuals with issues of narcissism as well as those who are dealing with narcissists in their lives and have had the privilege to witness the courage of these clients, as well as others, who engage in the work that can lead to satisfying transformational experiences, making for a healthy and more fulfilling quality of life.

Therefore, I am delighted to see that my colleague Richard Brouillette was so inspired by *Reinventing Your Life* that he decided to write a self-help book with the mission of offering readers the latest developments in schema therapy. I met Richard when he came to New Jersey to attend my training program, and I recognize the same warmth, humor, and down-to-earth tone in his writing that he brought to the classroom. Part of my work as a trainer involves helping clinicians to attune to their clients as human beings—to be "real" with them—and I recall Richard being particularly inspired by this notion. He shows up with a rare and rich authenticity and a robust connection to his reader. If this is your first experience with schema therapy, you've landed a great resource. This is a most meaningful contribution to the self-help reader as well as the therapist looking to understand this incredible treatment approach.

The full schema therapy approach involves a set of concepts, questionnaires, labels, and techniques that, taken together, can feel like a lot of moving parts for the newcomer. In this book, Richard skillfully distills the core themes of self-understanding, self-talk, solid behavior change, and self-compassion into accessible and user-friendly tools you can put into practice.

This book helps you understand the core concepts of schema therapy, as well as the strategies for change, and how schema therapy can work in a self-help context. You will learn how to connect difficult or painful challenging early life experiences with tough feelings, such as inadequacy, shame, anger, criticalness, or abandonment, and how these emotional beliefs lead to specific survival reactions—such as detachment, overcompensation, and compliant surrender—and how such patterns lead to frustration in the present moments. A schema therapist recognized these concepts as "schemas" and "modes," and Richard cleverly helps you to make sense of these beliefs and behaviors as they link with your "origin story."

The most innovative aspects of the book are those most practical. Each chapter pairs schema therapy concepts with exercises to put those ideas to use—whether you are learning more about your core needs, schemas, and modes, or practicing how to get in touch with and enhance your healthy caring adult mode. Richard shares exercises coming from the canon of schema therapy, including the use of a schema diary, the flash card, imagery, and chair work. But he adapts them for the self-help reader with skillful effort and thoughtfulness. His "mode theater" map is particularly handy as a memorable way to visualize parts of the self.

A schema therapist is always mindful of the need to bring the process back to helping their client make real and sustainable change in their life, and you'll find the same determination in this book. Everyday tools, including the use of your smartphone, will assist you in staying on track, with a focus on your goals, your healing destination. A core element of schema therapy is compassion and care for the self as part of the healing process, and in the final section of the book, Richard sensitively uses mindfulness techniques to help you make a practice of connecting to joy and care, keeping your motivational drivers alive and attuned.

If you are experiencing the challenges of self-defeating lifelong patterns and are looking for powerful tools to make real change, schema therapy offers that approach. And with this book, Richard will faithfully and creatively help you to cultivate healthy, adaptive coping skills that bring growth and change into your life in a meaningful, satisfying, and sustainable way.

—Wendy Behary, LCSW

How to Talk Yourself into Change

"What the hell is wrong with me?!" I'm sure you've said surprisingly negative stuff like this to yourself. You may find some of these classics familiar:

- "Why am I so lazy all the time? I'm the worst!"

- "I shouldn't say what I think; I'm lucky that anyone would be with me."

- "I never get the attention I need from my boyfriend, but there's no point in saying anything; that's just how it is for me."

When you say something like that to yourself, you're probably feeling and thinking it at the time. But if you're able to take a pause and step back, you may realize that you're not as bad as you're making yourself sound. Mean thoughts like these may be vocalizations of states of mind that ultimately, you don't even fully agree with. You may not like calling yourself lazy, telling yourself to stifle your needs or to stay in a job you don't like, or generally attacking yourself in a bid to cope with the things you're facing. "Oh, I was in a bad mood in that moment."

If people heard us say out loud the things that we say to ourselves, they would be shocked, right?

Often, we have mindsets that are supposed to help, but actually make things worse. So if you deal with self-sabotage and the experience of undermining your own progress, it may be that the coping skills that come most easily to you don't actually get you the results you want in your life. Consider this: we have unique mindsets that speak to us in strong voices, and they're *fighting* us on reaching our goals. Sometimes you may just notice the bad feeling, or sometimes you may hear the negative thought that goes with it, but either way, it's making life harder for you.

We all do it. It's funny that as human beings, we both assume that we are in charge of our lives—with free will—but we also see how often we don't exactly follow our own guidance or wishes. It can feel like we are at odds with ourselves, or even at war, with one side fighting to move in one direction while the other side is digging in and resisting. Just think about working out, or studying, or doing something hard. There is a communication breakdown with the self, and it builds until we're angrily saying to ourselves stuff like the above list. It always comes down to what we're saying to ourselves, how that talk moves us in the wrong direction, and how we may not even notice until after the damage is done. Sometimes we're our own unreliable narrator.

What does this look like in your everyday life? You may be pushing yourself hard in a super-demanding way, which just makes you angry and resentful all the time. You may avoid conflict and take on too much work rather than asserting yourself. You may spend your nights and weekends completely checked out from yourself and then feel bad Monday morning. You may just believe that you are incompetent and that you somehow get away with covering it up. You may feel like authority figures always treat you unfairly, then lash out at them, and get in trouble. You may feel that there's no point in trying, so you just push yourself along without motivation. You may feel completely baffled about what you really want, so your days feel empty. You may feel that people don't really like you, and you avoid them. You may feel like you have to work harder than everyone else or you'll be rejected.

So if you have these kinds of experiences, I'm going to show you how it's more than likely you're getting in your own way because of the difficult and painful self-talk you unleash. I'd like you to consider that if you adjust your perspective about self-talk, you can finally make positive change with less trouble. You can start *talking back*.

The key to overcoming personal obstacles is the idea that some part of you really thinks getting in your own way works. In other words, you have a set of coping reactions to personal challenges that really *feel* like they will help, but they don't at all. In fact, they're making things much worse. And this has likely been going on for a long time—since childhood.

I am going to help you hear when this mistaken part of you is talking and convince it to change. Another way to put it is: your coping skills aren't working, and you need to convince these "coping" parts of yourself to act in ways that are actually useful to you—by *talking* to them.

If what you hear in your head is, *Why am I so lazy all the time? I'm the worst!* then there is a problematic coping voice, or "schema," that's telling you, *I have to be this hard on myself to make a difference.* Or, if you think something like, *I shouldn't say what I think—I don't want to lose this relationship,* the schema you're struggling with is the belief *My needs are too much for people, and if I share them, I'll drive away the people I love.* The thought *I know I'm always the last person to leave the office, but if I don't work harder than everyone else, I'll get fired* reflects a schema—the belief *I have to work harder than everyone else or bad things will happen to me.* And the thought *I never get the attention I need from my boyfriend, but there's no point in saying anything*—which keeps you from communicating in the ways that might actually get your needs met—reflects a schema: the belief *People always let me down, so I have to protect myself by not setting myself up for disappointment.* And so on. These examples show

how negative thoughts *feel* like they have a helping message behind them, so we keep using them.

At a young age, we learned how to protect ourselves in ways that become obstacles when we're adults, but we get stuck with them. Here's what's really going on: Being too hard on yourself makes you miserable and less motivated. Not sharing your needs with people actually makes it hard for them to relate to you. Believing you have to work harder than everyone else distorts your outlook and leads to burnout and inefficiency. Avoiding vulnerability with people leads to perpetual disappointment.

The Foundation of This Book: Schema Therapy

This book refers to these problematic coping voices as "schemas" and will explore the ways that we cope with groups of schemas, called "modes"; how these perpetuate trouble; and how we can find a better way.

You will learn how your schemas and the ways you cope were often shaped by experiences you had when you were young. An overly critical inner voice may seem to serve you because, as a kid, you thought you had to live up to high standards and watch out for yourself. Or you may have an overly conciliatory voice that tells you it's better to let others have their way because when you were a kid, that helped you manage a domineering parent. If you have a voice telling you to be happy with what you've got and not strive for more, maybe you grew up emotionally neglected and learned it was easier to avoid getting your hopes for attention smashed once again.

Whatever the experiences that brought you here, I'll show you a unique way to address inner conflict: by taking the problematic coping voices seriously—recognizing their purpose may have served you at one time in your life and how they're holding you back now—and learning to talk back to those voices now that you're an adult who's able to cope with authority and agency.

This book approaches the idea of self-talk as healing via the lens of a school of psychotherapy called "schema therapy," as established by psychologist Jeffrey Young. This lens understands human psychology to be made up of schemas, which are triggered feelings and the particular core beliefs that they coalesce into, and modes, which are patterns of behavior that are shaped by our schemas.

We all have our individual map of the schemas and modes that makes us who we are—a map based a little bit on temperament, on our experience with emotional needs in childhood, and on the mix of care and neglect we had growing up. Schemas and modes offer a framework for understanding which parts of ourselves talk and which are painfully silenced, as well as where these parts came from, how they talk to each other, and how we can engage with what they say, want, and reveal in order to make change happen. Whoa, notice how I'm bringing more parts into the mix now? Once you get going with the schema therapy approach, the experience is challenging, lively, shockingly insightful, and deeply rewarding. Honestly, it can be fun at times too. When my therapy clients get the hang of working with the voices of different parts, they feel a new kind of effectiveness and freedom.

In the early nineties, the founder of the schema therapy method, Jeffrey Young, along with Janet Klosko, authored the book *Reinventing Your Life* (Young and Klosko 1993)—the original schema therapy self-help book. Young and Klosko showed us how to make sense of our history and ourselves with a simple core story: the way our needs were unmet in childhood tells us a lot about how we cope as adults and get in our own way. *Your Coping Skills Aren't Working* endeavors to honor the story Young and Klosko shared by expanding on it to include other schema therapy tools, like modes and additional experiential exercises. But it holds the same spirit of faith that you, the reader, armed with some helpful skills, can take yourself a very long way in overcoming your blocks.

As humans, we develop our coping skills in childhood as a way of coping with unmet emotional needs and our natural dependency. Children rely on their caregivers for a sense of right and wrong, conscience, guilt, and shame, but also for self-esteem, compassion for self and others, validation of their feelings and experience, and a solid belief that there is love in their world. There's a lot on the line.

The adults in children's lives act as a kind of external hard drive to help manage and build their personalities. If children lose that external help, or are shortchanged by it, they develop coping patterns that are often skewed. So, these coping patterns manifest as patterns of either relying too much on the self or putting too much on others. They stick around into adulthood. For example, maybe you *overcompensate*, promoting yourself as independent of others, not needing anyone, and working harder than everyone else; maybe you find yourself thinking it's weak or foolish to rely on others; or maybe you avoid asking much of others—sticking to your to-do list, possibly detaching from your emotions, and even detaching when you're alone, binge-watching TV or relying on food or substances to feel numb. You might end up *surrendering*—accepting without question what people say about you or feeling obligated to please people in order to get by—refraining from expressing your feelings or needs and trying to just fit into how others see the world (Young and Klosko 1993, 35–42).

Often, when we're adults, it becomes clear that *some* of these old ways of coping are no longer needed since we're no longer totally dependent on our parents and can take care of ourselves. We see that these skills are no longer useful because as adults, we're *expected* to be able to be independent and take care of ourselves. But we still hold on to other problematic coping skills. Why?

The answer lies in our understanding that our core emotions, like fear, joy, playfulness, abandonment, sadness, guilt, and love, all connect directly to our childhood experience. You could say these core emotions are a neurological direct line to parts of our brain linked to childhood. The coping skills we developed and hold onto were also formed during this period in childhood. So when we imagine letting go of core coping skills, we're talking about changing our relationship with core emotions, which is scary and makes us recoil. To really understand that fear, we have to put ourselves in the mindset of, say, a five-year-old child who is feeling vulnerable and defenseless. The fact is, we all still carry our own five-year-old inside.

Reaching for Vulnerability

Let's take a moment to get our feet wet with an imagery exercise (Behary 2019).

The imagery exercise is a tool we will be using together in-depth later in the book. For now, this is just a simple exercise to use your imagination to conjure up an image and see what emotions come up for you. It should only take a minute or two. Read the following scenario, and then give it a try. As you read the following imaginary scenario, if you think this exercise may be triggering for you, feel free to skip it.

Close your eyes, focus on your posture, straighten your spine, and plant your feet flat on the ground. Take a deep breath or two. Now clear you mind and find calm. When you feel at peace, let yourself imagine you are going for a walk in your neighborhood and that you see a five-year-old child across the street all alone. Fill in the description and details with your imagination. It becomes clear to you that this child is alone and lost. They don't know which way to turn and don't have anyone helping them. They see you and lock eyes with you. Okay, now freeze the frame in your mind and just hold on to the emotions you're experiencing. You are likely feeling some compassion for the child, perhaps you are wanting to help. (Other reactions are okay too!) But for now, focus on what the child is feeling. What must they be going through?

When you're ready, let that image fade out of your mind and let your mind go back to that calm, peaceful place free of images. Take a deep breath or two and open your eyes when you're ready.

What did the child feel? How was it to empathize with the child? What emotions and reactions do you imagine the child was going through? Chances are, they were feeling a lot of tough emotions, right? Panic, fear, abandonment, helplessness, and a really scary vulnerability and desperation. Completely defenseless.

Now think about how you may feel if you let go of all of your coping skills. You may be connecting with a lot of the same feelings that you imagined the child going through: defenseless, abandoned, vulnerable, and alone. This may be what it would feel like for you to think about dropping your ways of coping. Not so easy, right?

Ultimately, the prospect of letting go of our most ingrained coping skills—no matter how much we have faith in our adult selves—is scary and not something that happens overnight. We have to prove to our inner child that it's going to work, that our inner child can build trust in our adult self to take care. That takes time and practice.

(If you haven't let go of that image from our exercise, feel free to go back and help the child find their way home now!)

How This Book Will Help You Make Deep and Lasting Change

As we work on how you talk to yourself and ways you can talk back, I want to help expand your conception of what self-talk can be. Sometimes with a therapy client, I might ask something like, "If your anger could talk, what would it say?" Our self-talk can happen with emotions, feelings in our body, and unexpected behaviors and thoughts. So you will expand your fluency in understanding these different dialects and translating them back into self-awareness and conscious and productive self-talk in the service of connecting with the deepest parts of you—via your inner child.

Schema therapy is all about helping you find ways of living that connect with the inner child part of you, and all the other parts of you, to feel secure. To achieve this, we'll work simultaneously in the four areas of human experience: body, mind, emotions, and behavior. You will learn that the key to deep and lasting change comes from working in each of these areas and that these four elements of experience inform and nourish each other. It's a dance—or dialogue—of body, thoughts, feelings, and behavior intertwined and working off each other and looks something like this:

- Your *body* tells you what triggers you while your *mind* may be detached.

- When your *body* is triggered, your *thoughts* and mindset can help you calm down.

- You can rely on your *body signals* and *thoughts* to help change *behavior*.

- *Behavior change* improves your self-esteem, so you *feel* and *think* better of yourself.

- The better you *feel* and *think* about yourself, the more you can change, and on and on as a cycle.

Next, let's review these areas of experience in more detail. As you read, consider the unique ways your sense of self is impacted by each. Then, in the section that follows, you'll learn more about the schema therapy tools for each experience area.

Body experience. Do you feel low energy or a lack of motivation? Or are you overly tired and fatigued? Do you have trouble sleeping? Do you ever feel pressure in your chest? Do you get tense and jumpy or even panicky at times? These could all be signs of the schema-based fear you feel manifesting in your body.

In more everyday experience that isn't explicitly about symptoms, schema therapy also guides you to tune in to body experience when you're having thoughts or feelings about particular topics that might activate your schemas. For example, when you're thinking of a conflict you would rather avoid, what do you feel in your body? Very often it's pressure in the chest.

Cognitive experience. In terms of symptoms, are you having negative or worrying thoughts that become obsessive, cycling, and hard to stop? Do you have thoughts that are overly judgmental of others or self-critical? Do you find you have baseline negative beliefs about relationships, such as whether people like you or whether you can trust people? These thoughts and beliefs come from the schemas you hold. They drive the symptoms you feel and limit what you're able to do. Tracking thoughts and beliefs and the effects they have on you is a hallmark of the cognitive behavioral therapy (CBT) approach—and it will help you learn to change them.

Emotional experience. Do you feel waves of sadness without knowing exactly why? Do you have a hard time letting go of grief? Do you find that you become noticeably angry without knowing why? Or are you feeling absence of emotion and numbness? Is loneliness an issue, where you have a hard time enjoying your own company? Emotions are often a signpost to memories of other times that were formative for you, but possibly forgotten.

Behavioral experience. Do you procrastinate in a way that is interfering with success? Are you avoidant of things you should be doing? Do you engage in lot of numbing or detaching behavior, like binge-watching? Do you think you may be abusing substances or food or overly preoccupied with dieting and working out—and that these behaviors are operating as a distraction from something, rather than being ends in themselves? Are you isolating? You will learn how problematic behaviors are often signs that can help you identify what is troubling you and how to introduce new behaviors to help change thoughts and feelings.

Ultimately, with this holistic, four-dimension approach, you will learn how to create a *dialogue* among all four dimensions of your experience. This way, change you make in one dimension will influence change in the other three.

The Tools You Will Learn in This Book

This book is essentially your schema therapy toolbox. In this book, you will learn a set of terms to understand yourself, techniques for learning more about what you think and feel, new ways to communicate with yourself, solid skills for making behavior change, and a new appreciation for compassion, joy, and kindness.

The tools you will learn encompass the holistic four-dimension approach and will include:

- writing exercises and journaling
- "self-portrait" exercises with photos
- imagery work
- mode dialogues
- diary cards and flash cards
- using a planner and notifications
- mindfulness meditation.

You can download worksheets from website for this book at http://www.newharbinger.com/50997. I'd also like you to have a notebook or journal to use as you go through this book. It will be helpful to have one place to look back on the work you've done, as each chapter builds on the last. Make the journal large enough so you can use it for a couple of months of daily journaling. Some folks like to pick a journal that's pleasing and special to build motivation. Others find that intimidating and just get a spiral bound notebook. Do whatever you like.

Using these tools, I'll teach you how to create a dialogue among all four dimensions of experience. This way, change in one dimension influences change in the other three. It's also true that only approaching change in a single dimension—for example, the cognitive experience—will actually result in the other three dimensions *working against* any progress made with just thoughts. This often undermines your effort to change, making it repetitive and exhausting. So, while certain tools will make the most impact with certain dimensions of experience, they're meant to be used together to foster successful change and growth in all four dimensions. But before we get started, I want you to know that, with this book, I'm putting *all* the tools on the table for you, which may seem like a lot. So just work with what you can at your own pace, and you'll do great!

You Are Not Alone

Schema therapy as a process is about learning how to be present with the different parts that make up the whole that is you: child and adolescent you from different points on the timeline of your life, the different mindsets and feelings that make up complicated you in the present, and your wishes and visions of who you want to be in the future. When Future You finishes this book, my hope is that you are truly compassionate and caring for all your parts and images. When you do, you'll never feel alone again.

One of the key qualities of a schema therapist is to be honest, forthcoming, and authentic with clients and avoid "sounding like a therapist," which means using a kind of "it sounds like you are sad" tone that can be distancing and overly neutral. You're going to get authentic me as the author of this book and your guide through this process.

I know you came to this book for very real and serious concerns that you're trying to overcome. I'm asking a lot of you by having you stick to the routine and exercises in this book, and I understand that if you do so, you are trusting me with your time and have faith that this program will be a success for you. I won't forget this as we go through the book together.

Yes, together. As I write this now and you read it now, I want you to feel that you are exactly the person I wrote this book for. Maybe think of this book in your hand as the only copy in existence and that I wrote it with you in mind because that's how I intend it. Every time a therapist starts with a new client, the therapist needs to have a "beginner's mind" and approach that client with the understanding that they are unlike any other, the problems and strengths they bring to the world are unique, and the therapy is the first step in an adventure. I've designed this book to help you to experience your full uniqueness, strengths, creativity, and challenges in an authentic way. As we go, I want you to keep in mind the image that I am right here with you, cheering you on, helping you stay accountable, and offering sympathy and support. Because I am.

So let's do this!

Chapter 1

Troublesome Coping Skills and the Self-Esteem Solution

Your first experience of having difficulty with behavior or thoughts and feelings may just be feeling stuck, a feeling that, no matter how you try to change, the same problems keep happening. It's like a merry-go-round. It gets so frustrating that it leads to a feeling of helplessness or to avoidance, detachment, bitterness, or cynicism, and worse. So we're going to start this chapter with three people's stories of being stuck. Getting an outsider's view on stuckness can help you gain a new perspective on yourself. I'll use these stories to also introduce schema concepts.

Meet Eddie, Judy, and Ze

Eddie had a problem with working too much. He would spend long hours at his desk, and by the time he let himself finish for the day, he had a hard time relaxing, always feeling guilty about not doing more or better. In the evening, he would lose himself online or binge-watch TV, which were his preferred ways of getting his mind off his worries. He had a hard time with dating, as he would spend a lot of time obsessing about someone's online profile, whether to contact them, how he should do it, and so on. Worrying got in the way of taking action and sending a message. With both work and dating, Eddie felt like he needed to prepare more so he would succeed. Sometimes he would try to relax, not to worry, and to be spontaneous. But it would make him too nervous and worry even more, and he would return to obsessively anticipating problems and preparing. The more frustrated he got, the more he would check out at night and detach. He started to feel ashamed of his lack of progress, wouldn't get support from friends and family, and started isolating.

To her friends, Judy appeared to be a truly kind and competent person, though a little rigid and hard to get close to. She could even be charming. Judy was aware that she could be defensive but felt that it was somehow difficult to trust people. When talking to friends or colleagues, she was usually a bit uncomfortable and thinking about how to end the discussion and get away. When chatting, she found that she was guarded and didn't want to share too much. She imagined people judging her, rejecting her, even laughing at her, or just feeling sorry for her. She felt if she showed too much of herself, people would see "what a loser" or "how pathetic" she really was. So she did her best to have a good life, keep friendships, and be successful in her career. She isolated herself a lot and sometimes drank alone. Judy told herself the way out of this was to have more social time and get closer to people. But the more she tried, the more exhausted she got with trying to conceal her true self.

Ze was active in their community and very driven by social justice and attending to and defending oppressed people. Ze had been bullied when they were young and learned the lesson that it's better not to trust people—it's safer that way. Ze often felt like they were caring for an emotional bruise underneath and had to treat themselves with caution, avoid risks, and isolate. While they were well-respected, they usually felt like they had to go along with the flow, provide people what they want, and never really speak up for their own needs. This left Ze feeling resentful or angry and neglected, which they usually expressed on behalf of others in their activism, rather than in their personal life. Ze tried to help themself by moving in the direction of being more self-sufficient, stronger, and more independent. They were good at this, but it didn't change the feelings of loneliness and vulnerability.

Like Eddie, Judy, and Ze, you too may know you want to change, but how do you know *what* to change? In other words, what is the problem, and what is the solution?

With each of the above composite examples of people and their problems, you can see some behaviors that clearly need to change, such as working too much, keeping people at a distance, self-isolating, and not trusting others. There's no denying that these behavior patterns make each person frustrated, alone, and unhappy. Each person could focus on trying to change their behavior—for example working less and getting closer to people—but they would each also face the challenge of strong feelings telling them to keep doing the behavior they want to stop. "You have to work harder; you have to prove yourself in order to stay safe in this world!" "It would be great to get closer to people, but they hurt you, and you can't trust them!" We could consider these deeper core beliefs to be the motivators for the negative behavior these folks are trying to change.

Often people feel friction when trying to change a behavior because they're trying to change the behavior without addressing the core belief that drives the behavior. The result is that the change process becomes incredibly fatiguing because by changing their behavior, they're also trying to force themselves to act against what they believe reality is. It's like grinding gears. Imagine not knowing how to swim and every day standing by the deep end of the pool and saying, "I just have to jump in, and I will swim fine." Underneath, your brain and body are telling you "Danger!" and you can't ignore those signals. You sense how difficult behavior change can be if you don't take on both the behavior and core belief underlying it.

Okay, so far, so good. Once we know the behavior we want to change and the belief behind the behavior, we just need to do a reality check on that belief and change it so it's then easier to change the behavior, right? Well, kind of.

If someone has a deeply held belief about how relationships or the world works, how easy is it to convince them their belief is wrong? Here's a hint: it's not easy! It's really hard. People often spend their whole lives with these strong beliefs, and they have navigated themselves into adulthood using them. They're not so easy to change through argument or "reality checking."

Think about Eddie, Judy, and Ze, our case studies above. Each has deeply held beliefs about how to survive in the world: Eddie believes he has to work harder than everyone else, Judy believes that she is defective somehow and needs to shelter herself from people's judgments, and Ze was bullied in their youth and has some very real experiences that prove people hurt you if you get too close to them. In fact, they each likely had childhood experiences that cemented their survival skills early. So it may be very difficult indeed to convince them that their beliefs about safety and survival are wrong.

Schema therapy offers a solution to this dilemma. It allows us to connect to the childhood roots of deeply held beliefs—to answer the questions: What are these beliefs I hold? Where did they come from in the first place?—and then offers compassion in response: *These beliefs come from your childhood experiences, from your child-self. It makes sense you felt that way at the time and learned how to cope the way you did. But those days are over, and life can be different now.*

Ultimately, it comes down to two things: compassion for the childhood self and dialogue with that self. In the context of dealing with coping skills, this means understanding and having compassion for why the coping skills were necessary in the first place and then having a dialogue with the part of the self that still feels vulnerable so you can see the truth of your situation as it stands now. Then you can decide what you want to do as an adult to live in a way you truly value, rather than doing what an old childhood fear or long-hardened instinct tells you to do.

Compassion for and Dialogue with the Inner Child

From a schema therapy perspective, the source of our coping skills and core beliefs is childhood experience, specifically how we, as children, coped with unmet core emotional needs.

Why do these childhood experiences still affect us and our behavior? From a neuropsychological perspective, essentially, we have an ongoing relationship with the trauma of having our emotional needs unmet; the pain we felt at the time becomes a kind of *lesson learned*. The pain is imprinted in our brain, reminding us that we have to behave a certain way in order to avoid further hurt. So the sum of our difficult childhood experience is still with us in the present, and we are still using the same coping skills we developed back then.

This is the inner child part of ourselves. We all have one, and it's been with us since birth, holding emotions, beliefs, and memories that were created before our subconscious was able to process what was going on. When we talk about the inner child, we're talking about an image of our child-self that helps us connect with our early unmet needs more consciously.

Imagining a composite image of our inner child is a practical and effective technique to understand our needs because we're relating to an image of a person. By imagining our inner child, we are also reminding ourselves that our emotional needs from that period are simple and based on being cared for by others, literally childlike. Children don't have autonomy or independence as adults do, so they must rely on their caregivers completely with utter dependence.

This is why compassion and dialogue are necessary for personal transformation. When we are being compassionate with ourselves, we are in dialogue with the inner child who needs to know they are being cared for by someone with authority and power. This adult-child dynamic is the core of how schema therapy helps overcome problematic coping skills.

What tough feelings do you recall from your childhood? These tough feelings will likely tell you about some unmet needs you had and how you felt you "had to do it on your own," when there were no adults willing or able to help. Doing it on your own at the time meant trying to get by in an adult world and live by the adults' rules, however fair they were—or not. Doing it on your own meant trying to manage without any validation or support from a parent. So in the schema therapy approach, we finally see what the inner child went through, validate the inner child, and offer compassion for how they got through. And then we tell that inner child, "Look, you're an adult now, and you get to make new rules!"

Did you feel really scared and alone at night (abandonment schema)? You may have found a way to tolerate feeling alone and scared because you didn't really have a choice, but now as an adult, maybe there are times when you feel intensely alone and scared and aren't sure why.

Did you feel like you had to accomplish things by yourself, otherwise you felt shame (unrelenting standards schema)? You may have been in over your head getting through your day without enough support or guidance from an adult. So the stakes of messing up were high because it felt like no one would save you. You were in a position of trying to do things you were not ready or able to do because you weren't old enough. Now as an adult, perhaps you still feel like the stakes are high when you do work, and you overdo it.

Did you feel like you couldn't do things "correctly" (failure schema)? You may have had caregivers who weren't so good at remembering that children have to learn to do things and, that depending on their age, are not neurologically ready for certain tasks. So they made unfair demands on their children, which can leave kids feeling like they are just bad at doing things. And that feeling can stick into adulthood.

Did you feel like you had to take care of your parents or siblings and put them first (self-sacrifice schema)? Often children are unfairly placed in a caregiving role, either for siblings or even parents. This situation takes the child's focus off the lessons of growing up, including playing, learning, and experiencing emotions unburdened. Instead, a caregiving child must take on worry for others' welfare and will feel guilty about having their own needs. This guilt about having your own needs can stick into adulthood as a schema.

Schemas are born out of a child's hardship of feeling helpless when the adults fall short. That schema pain stays with us neurologically into adulthood, and we're still waiting for an adult to step in and care, and we're still trying to cope without the right tools. But as adults, we can provide the care that has been lacking over the years by providing ourselves compassion and dialogue. As adults, we have the power to fully address our unmet needs.

Note that I am not saying everyone was traumatized in childhood. But everyone has schemas. No one grows up with their emotional needs fully met 100 percent of the time, and the schemas form in the areas of need that are not at all or not fully addressed. This is a kind of shaping of our individual personalities and helps us develop our character and become the person we are, strengths, talents, warts, and all.

Schema therapists don't just view schemas as problems to be removed but honor them as the best solution child-you could come up with at the time. Those schemas got you where you are now and helped you survive. But it's also important to accept that your coping skills may have become so "effective" that you don't remember what it's like to have emotional needs or get them fulfilled. When that happens, it's like your "new normal," which is what leads to stuckness, lack of fulfillment, detachment, relationship trouble, loneliness, anger, and even anxiety, depression, and other mental health issues. The thing is, we really don't want to let go of habitual coping skills because we feel naked and vulnerable without them, so we get stuck in a vicious cycle.

What It Means to Have Unmet Emotional Needs

Eddie grew up with high-achiever parents, his mother, a health care executive and father, a corporate lawyer. His parents were preoccupied with their careers in a way that left Eddie in the care of nannies and babysitters until he later spent time alone after school most days. Being African American, Eddie learned from his parents early on that in order to make it, he had to be the best at everything in order to overcome institutional racism. His parents believed they were showing their love to Eddie by having high standards for him without offering much affection. This combination of high standards and emotional coldness left Eddie to conclude that he was only loveable if he performed well. The racism he encountered as he got older only reinforced what his parents told him.

The focus of Eddie's experience growing up in the care of his parents was on performance. In a very understandable way, his parents took care of him by ensuring he could handle the tough and unfair world that was waiting for him. One can certainly read love in this approach. In fact, Eddie's adult life and career success are a tribute to his parents' approach. But in Eddie's adult life, we can see evidence of what was lacking for him as a child. In Eddie's childhood, there was little tenderness, loving encouragement, or forgiveness. One of his core emotional needs was to know that if he made mistakes, or had a learning curve, it was okay and that he was still loved. He was never quite sure of that, so he never developed a sense of self-worth beyond proof by performance.

The main question for Eddie is: How does one disconnect love from the transactional idea of performance?

As for Judy, growing up, most of the attention she received was from her mother, as her father was detached and made himself busy with work or hobbies in a way that he was mostly absent. Judy's mother unfortunately believed that harshness was the best form of love for her child to prepare her for the world. If Judy made mistakes or needed to be taught how to do something, her mother would yell or use an exasperated, impatient tone. This left Judy believing that there must be something wrong with her. Should she know more things or just be better at doing things? Why wasn't she better, more capable?

Sadly, Judy carried a strong feeling of poor self-worth from childhood into her adult life. Because her father was mostly emotionally absent and her mother used an exasperated and at times contemptuous tone with her, Judy received the repeated message that there was something wrong with her. *How could I make these mistakes? Why is my mother so impatient with me? Why doesn't my father talk to me? I must have done something wrong, or maybe I'm just wrong.*

Of course, there wasn't any guarantee she'd get a sympathetic ear from her parents if she ever expressed any of these feelings. So, Judy also developed a strong instinct to keep that supposedly defective part of her hidden to protect herself.

As a child, Judy needed to know that she would be accepted and loved no matter how well she performed (within realistic limits). Instead, the repeated message that she "did things wrong"—that she, in some way, *was* wrong—left her need for unconditional love unfulfilled. As an adult, Judy juggled a hidden internal belief that she was flawed and a failure with an external life of being highly competent with an intense isolating fortitude that discouraged her from sharing parts of herself that she worried would be seen as weak.

Ze was raised in a busy environment. The youngest of four children, Ze's parents were rigid and conservative with emotion and praise, and they focused on showing care for the children by being demanding about grades. Beyond the focus on performance in school, however, Ze's parents largely left their children to their own devices. Ze would get some support and attention from an older sister, but they were often neglected or treated poorly by their other siblings. Ze believed the best approach to life was to stay under the radar to avoid any mistreatment. Ze also came to believe that their self-esteem was safe if they just avoided attention. This made it hard for them to know how to stand up for themselves when they encountered conflict and people who violated their boundaries—which is inevitable at times for everyone. These tendencies left Ze vulnerable to bullying as they grew up, which further engrained the belief that "if you get close to people, they hurt you."

Ze grew up with the core beliefs that people by their nature are hurtful, that Ze will be deeply wounded if they allow people close, and that it's better to "stay under the radar" at a personal level to avoid being hurt. Ze, as all children do, had a fundamental need for a sense of safety and security that they could take for granted, a need to be able to trust that their parents kept their well-being in mind and cared about them, and a need to trust that their siblings were also essentially loving.

As we consider these stories, remember we are looking at the behaviors each person wants to change and how those behaviors are linked to core beliefs, which in turn came out of an experience of unmet needs in childhood. Here's the thing: Very young children are smart and know at an intuitive level what they need emotionally. They are very aware of the pretzels they bend themselves into in order to preserve relationships with caregivers. But there's often not much they can do about the *fact* that they have to preserve relationships with their caregivers. So, part of the process of coping with the bind they find themselves in—where they're not getting what they need from the people who care for them and whom they depend on to survive—is to let this conflict go, forget it, block it out, or dissociate it.

In the same way, by returning to the situations that speak to your unmet emotional needs—as you're doing now—you are opening up unfinished business between you and the caregivers who let you down in some way, whether or not they meant to. You're in the process of asking, "What did I need, and what was reasonable and fair of me to expect, which I was denied?"

The schema therapy approach is to use compassion for the inner child and dialogue with the inner child to reconnect with your unfinished business so you can validate your needs and reopen yourself to fulfilling them. In this way, you will be able to access the source of the behavior you want to change.

We can frame this unfinished business as a script, or piece of dialogue, Eddie, Judy, and Ze might have with their own inner child.

In Eddie's case, his script might go something like this: "It's okay to love and respect your parents, to be thankful for what they did for you, and to accept that they fell short in certain ways. You needed more love and affection than you got from them. That doesn't mean you didn't deserve it. It means they fell short. You deserve love just for being you, as you are."

As for Judy, her script might be: "I know you believe your parents did their best with you and that they love you, and I'm sure that's true. But nobody's perfect, and some of their parenting skills sold you short and left you feeling badly about yourself. You needed to know that you were a good kid, that you were smart and capable, that you tried hard, and that you were loved just for being you."

Finally, Ze's script might go as follows: "You deserved to grow up in a family that could pay enough attention to you so you would never have to worry about being safe. As a kid, you should only have had to focus on being a kid. You shouldn't have had to think about your safety or wonder whether anyone would be there for you when you needed them. And when you were bullied, you needed someone to tell you it wasn't your fault and that you deserved to be safe. You needed someone to defend you from bullies or help you stand up to them because you matter. Now that you're an adult, you can come to terms with the unfairness of the past and help yourself understand that things are different now and that you have the good judgment to choose to know and love people who care for you and who won't hurt you."

Meeting Your Needs and Building Real Self-Esteem

Compassionate dialogue with yourself—the same kind you just saw Eddie, Judy, and Ze engage in—is the way to build self-esteem that overcomes the need for maladaptive coping skills. Building self-esteem starts with creating the validation, support, and care that you did not experience so well in childhood. It doesn't mean not needing others; it doesn't mean being entirely alone. It means building a new relationship with yourself—having the ability to see and be in dialogue with your inner child so it can tell you not just what it needs, but what would be joyous, what would make it happy, and how to be creative—so you can be a healthy, self-confident adult and do the things you really want to do.

This is what schema therapists would call the *healthy caring adult mode*. Note this doesn't mean rejecting your child-self. After all, many of our problematic coping skills are a result of rejecting the pain and vulnerability of childhood. It can feel counterintuitive, but it's actually by moving toward childhood vulnerability that we learn how to care for our inner child—at which point, we let its ways of coping go; they are no longer necessary. When you do this, you'll become more sensitive to your own deep feelings and more confident in your ability to attend to those needs so you can live life as you truly wish to live it.

In that spirit, let's look at the way childhood vulnerability manifests: the specific schemas we might develop to deal with the needs that have gone unmet and the specific patterns of behavior, or modes, that result.

Schemas and Modes: The Building Blocks of Your Personality

One of the most effective elements of schema therapy is how it uses the power of naming. As we begin to name the different patterns of emotional triggering (schemas) and coping responses (modes) that make up the personality, we can start to get some distance from ourselves, and we have an opportunity for a new perspective and a different kind of self-awareness. You'll start to think about how you want to be different with a real sense of openness. It's a lot like using the theory of DNA to understand our particular genome and how it makes us tick.

As you start putting together a picture of your schemas and modes, you'll do it by reading the story of your childhood with compassion and empathy. Once you know what you're looking for, you will see cues of unmet needs, the schemas that form from unmet needs, and then the modes that develop as ways of coping and behaving. By looking at your coping skills this way, you can approach your story differently. You'll be able to read your own story a bit like reading a novel that means a lot to you. You'll really care about what happens to the main character and feel their loss, pain, and needs with sympathy and understanding. Instead of Charles Dickens or Toni Morrison, you'll be reading the story of your own life. Needs, schemas, and modes are the tools that will help.

As you read the novel of you, keep in mind it's a story about emotional needs and how they change over time. We start as infants, utterly dependent on others to survive with a great need for unconditional love. As we grow and improve at being independent and meeting our own needs, we need the room to do so and to make mistakes knowing someone is there to pick us up with care, accountability, and limit-setting. In adolescence, we need to know we're working without a net on the way to adulthood. The evolution of our emotional needs is really a story of the evolution of our self-esteem. But the key to the story is in the early years when schemas form, around birth to age five, the period when we need unconditional love. Then, from age five to ten, our schemas start to pattern our behavior into modes, especially as we are socializing in school and our brain develops.

The Goal Is Self-Acceptance

As you go through this process, don't forget that out of schemas and modes also come your strengths. The silver lining of the challenge of these problematic coping skills is that there are terrific, unique aspects of your character that you value, whether they are smarts, ambition, creativity, or sensitivity.

This is an important idea that can easily get lost in all the talk about "change" and "coping" in the mental health world: the ultimate goal is self-acceptance. There may be aspects of our experience and reactions that we would like to change because we sense they aren't serving us well or they don't reflect the people we really want to be. But at our core, we have a character that is uniquely ours—and this character inevitably has more strengths and valuable qualities than "flaws." This regard for ourselves—as valuable as we are, with many strengths and much to offer—is a kind of self-acceptance that echoes the unconditional love we all needed as young children. And it's the key to changing behavior.

In the end, when you think about those parts of yourself you want to get rid of, remember they are probably connected to some of your strengths, and remember to treat yourself with kindness. You really deserve it.

In this chapter, you discovered the paradigm shift that schema therapy can offer when you're stuck in a pattern of self-sabotage and self-defeat—the ways you typically cope aren't working for you, but you're unsure exactly what to do about it or how to fix it. By looking at Eddie's, Judy's, and Ze's stories, you came to see how much we can "get in our own way" and make our problems worse with our coping skills—because those coping skills helped us deal with the pain we experienced in childhood, but they may not be the best ways of getting our needs met in adulthood.

This insight—that it's our own coping skills and core beliefs about ourselves that leave us trapped or stuck in self-sabotaging patterns—can be difficult to fully accept, as our coping skills are so deeply engrained. But again, while it's contradictory, the way to really change is by accepting the things that we want to change and by having compassion for them first. We naturally develop a negative attitude toward what we see as flaws or as the ways we fall short, sometimes even hating them. But the only way we can really overcome them is letting go of that negativity and using acceptance. With a foundation of acceptance, we are no longer fighting ourselves—which is the source of our stuckness.

Chapter 2

Your Origin Story: Unmet Core Emotional Needs

The core emotional needs are really the source of your "origin story," which is the story of how you came to be you. Most superheroes have an origin story involving loss, unmet needs, and trauma, which add heart and soul to the character but also complexity of internal conflict. Think about Superman, an exile from another planet, who has normal human parents, but also lost his birth parents from his home planet. The X-Men are exiled or profiled from their particular communities due to their powers. Spiderman was orphaned, as was Batman. Or think of Scrooge from *A Christmas Carol,* who was neglected as a boy by a stern father and left at boarding school alone every Christmas. These experiences of loss give each character meaning and become a way in for the audience to identify with them.

Your Origin Story of Five Core Emotional Needs

Let's take the same approach with you. How do you understand your own origin story? You may first react to that question by thinking of your family, the personality of your parents, the place you grew up, or your religion, cultural background, or interests. All of these things are relevant to who you are, but in this context, we are looking at the origin story that created who you are in terms of how you are in relationships, how you show emotion, how much entitlement you feel, how assertive you are, and your state of self-esteem. We are looking at the origin story of how you experience your core emotional needs (Young et al. 2003, 9–10).

If you can figure out the *why* of the things you tend to do, the habits, and the coping strategies you tend to default to—which of your core emotional needs have been met and which haven't—you may be able to get a better grip on your life going forward.

As we grow up and observe our parents, family, relationships, and society, we are constantly coming up with theories to explain how we get what we need and how things work. But crucially, during the early period of childhood, we are using a brain that isn't yet fully developed, so the logic we use is often skewed. A well-known example of this child logic is how a child of divorce often blames himself for his parents splitting up, "If only I wasn't naughty, they would still be together."

But as we explain to ourselves why things happen, these explanations harden into deeply held beliefs about ourselves in the world. These are the stories that stick with us into adulthood. For us, the story is always about our unmet core emotional needs. We come into this world dependent on others, with urgent physical and emotional needs. From birth, the question of whether these needs are met is a matter of life and death. *That is real drama and suspense.* If you're a hungry child, waiting to find out when you're going to eat next adds a real sense of meaning to your life. It's the same experience of having the need to be recognized as a person with feelings, however young you are.

Schema therapists understand the plot of your life by analyzing the story of your unmet core emotional needs, which determine the schemas you form—the patterns of memories, emotions, and behavior that you follow throughout your lifetime. Let's take a look at the five core emotional needs now.

Five Core Emotional Needs

From newborns crying when they are hungry, through breastfeeding in infancy and bed-sharing in early childhood, to the experiences of late childhood and adolescence, there is a nexus of human need, emotion, and communication happening. Ultimately, feeling need and expressing discomfort through feelings are how we survive, as we are utterly dependent on our caregivers. So the feelings we have are both a form of self-awareness and a means to communicate our needs to others— needs that are sometimes met, and sometimes not. We are always having a dialogue between our needs and our environment—one that, as we age, shapes our instinctive responses to our experiences and our behaviors.

Schema therapy establishes five core needs, as listed below (Young et al. 2003, 10). You can think of each of the five needs as the second part of a sentence that begins "You deserve to have…"

- Safety, love, and care

- Self-confidence and sense of identity

- Validated feelings and needs

- Loving discipline and limits

- Joy, playfulness, and creativity.

Schema therapists look at all the stages of human growth—which stretches through and includes infancy, early childhood, middle school and junior high, adolescence, and young adulthood—through the lens of these core emotional needs. They look at the ways unmet needs predispose clients to form certain schemas that go on to inform their behavior in particular ways.

Some needs take a priority during certain ages. For example, the need for safety is fundamental and particularly formative in infancy; having your feelings validated is crucial in early toddlerhood; having loving discipline and limit-setting are crucial in the years that follow. Next, self-confidence and having a sense of identity become more important, and creative self-expression becomes crucial during socialization. But all five needs are important and remain important, regardless of age, as part of human development. So in early childhood, a child may need to feel that they are the center of the world in their parents' eyes, but during adolescence, a young person may need to prove their individuality and act out with parents, while the parents hopefully aspire to tolerate these unpleasant challenges with love, support, and understanding and, at the same time, maintain safe and fair limits.

If your own core emotional needs were not met across the stages of your lifespan, you developed coping skills to compensate for those unmet needs. And depending on how it goes, your coping skills can ultimately hurt more than they help. But that's true of all for us, and it is part of the origin story we each have. It is who we are with strengths and weaknesses.

I like to think of the five core emotional needs as the DNA of human need: the source from which all other needs derive, the wellspring of how we feel and express our core selves, and how we relate to each other. Consider these needs as urgent and necessary as any physical needs, like the need for air, food, water, and shelter. We all have these needs, and we are all born into a particular set of circumstances that allow for or inhibit these needs being met. And when your core needs went unmet or you met them the best way you knew how at the time, the result is the development of certain schemas that dictate how you behave in the face of circumstances you encounter to this day.

Think of a kid who develops asthma growing up in an area with auto or factory pollution. This child had the need for clean, breathable air, but was born into circumstances that met this core need with severe externally imposed limitations, and the result is an ongoing set of breathing issues due to the original need only partially being met. It's the same with the core emotional needs. As children, we're born with the need for safe, loving, and caring relationships with caregivers. But if your parents were neglectful or abusive, you may have developed a coping mode of detaching or dissociating as a way of blocking out all the hurtful aspects of living with your caregivers because as a child, you had no other choice.

Another way to look at core needs is simply to ask: Did our caregivers arrange for us, as children, to have all we needed so we could devote as much of our attention as possible to the business of just growing up?

How much was this true of your childhood? Ultimately, we all fall on a spectrum in that we probably got some needs met and others not. The poignant and even heartbreaking aspect of childhood is that we do what we must psychologically in order to hold on to the idea of having the caring parent that we need. There really isn't a return policy on the parents we get and the cards we're dealt.

But there are things we can do now to identify the needs that went unmet in our childhood and get them met now, in better ways than we did when we were children. In order to get a better sense of your origin story and the challenges you faced getting your own needs met, here's an experiential exercise to bring those childhood core emotional needs back into focus. While you sharpen your sensibility around your origin story and unmet needs, you will also be deepening your self-compassion. As you build this new self-awareness, you will be opening yourself up to making profound change.

Exercise: Getting to Know "Little You," Part 1

Find a photo of yourself as a kid that you can work with. The ideal age would be around five, and it can be a family photo or a school photo (Behary 2019). (If for some reason you don't have access to a childhood photo, you can imagine yourself as a child at this age.) Now put aside some time to spend with the photo, in a private place with no interruptions, for about thirty minutes. Be ready to do some writing. As you consider your photo, write down your answers to the following questions:

1. As you're looking at Little You, what thoughts are going through your mind? Try to be as honest with yourself as you can here. Sometimes this exercise can surprise us with negative reactions. That's okay. We can also surprise ourselves with our own compassion toward that little kid we're looking at. Go where you go.

2. Looking at the photo, what emotions are coming up for you right now, and where do you feel those emotions in your body? For example, is there a pressure in your chest or a feeling in your throat or in your gut?

3. What was going on for Little You at the time this photo was taken? I'll ask you a few questions to get your mind going, but don't worry if it's hard to recall much detail. Earlier childhood memories can be difficult to pull up. Sometimes little details are a bread-crumb trail to bigger memories. What was it like at home? How were your parents or caregivers with you? What was the temperature of their care for you like: hot, warm, cold? Who else were you close to? How did you sleep at night? How did it go when you had bad dreams or were afraid of the dark? Did anyone read stories to you? What toys, games, or shows did you like? Did you have a favorite food or treat? Favorite holidays?

Remember, you are looking at a snapshot of your story, of being a kid just trying to get through life and do the work of growing up. While using a childhood photo of oneself is a technique used in different schools of psychotherapy, Wendy Behary introduced a unique application of the childhood photo in schema therapy, particularly in her efforts to help narcissistic clients connect with their vulnerability, although it turns out to work very well for most people, narcissistic or not (Behary 2013, 149).

So as Adult You visiting Little You, did you get a sense of unmet needs and what your origin story may be? Later in this chapter, you'll have the opportunity to go deeper to answer that question.

First, though, we'll look at the five core emotional needs all children have and why they are crucial in the schema therapy approach. So we are going to take a bit of a detour before we come back to this exercise with fresh eyes and more background information on what we're doing.

Considering the Five Core Emotional Needs in Detail

As you read the following descriptions of the five core emotional needs, I want you to reflect on how you experienced each need growing up. I'll ask some questions to nudge your thinking along the way. Some of what you read and consider here may be heavy; take your time with it, take care of yourself as you read, and know that the exploration you do now is in the service of helping you build a better life in the future.

Safety, Love, and Care

The idea of safety here is broad and applies to both the physical and emotional dimensions. When you were a child, you needed to know that your environment was safe from actual danger, that there was nothing and no one to be afraid of, and that you and everyone around you were safe and unworried. Children can sense fear and worry in others and take it on. Safety is also important in a physical sense, especially as a child's field of activity widens with growth. From the room they were in as an infant to the street where they played when they were preschool age, they needed to be free of fear. And of course, safety is also important when it comes to the safety of caregivers. The experience of domestic violence is particularly relevant. The direct experience of violence in the household can be a grievous one; children can see violence done to others and take it in as though it may happen to them, not to mention feel the anguish of seeing a loved one hurt.

Care, too, is a dimension of physical and emotional safety. Children need to feel cared for, whether with loving words or attention to their physical comfort. Just as children can sense worry, they can also sense when others care.

At an emotional dimension, when you were growing up, did you experience safety and care in your world? Were you free from violent anger and mean or sadistic treatment? Unfortunately, humanity has a sad history and inclination to treat children like objects without emotions, as though their experience doesn't need to be treated sensitively. Ever hear the expression "children should be seen and not heard"? But children are always aware of more than adults give them credit for. Always. Experiences of harm and violence register for them. At a more subtle level, children are sensitive to tone and can feel when they are being treated with contempt, harshness, or even taunting.

As you will see throughout this book, people need things put into words. It can't only be implied or assumed that a parent loves a child; it needs to be said with words and physical affection. Children need to know that they are loved. They crave to learn language so they can express and accept love, and they are motivated by being told they are loved. They deserve the experience of learning how to tell someone else "I love you" and opportunities to say it and hear it.

Take a moment to journal about your experience with this need in the present. How much do you allow yourself to rely on others to feel safety, love, and care? How much do you find you are able to provide a feeling of safety, love, and care for yourself? How did you experience safety, love, and care growing up?

Self-Confidence and Sense of Identity

Have you ever encountered a four-year-old who gets angry when you try to do something for them? "I wanna do it!" There's probably some temperament coming out there, but there's also the clear need a child has to learn how to do things for themself. A funny variation is certainly when a kid picks out their clothes for the day. These can be delicate choices for a parent to make, regarding how they allow their child to express themselves within the bounds of creativity and autonomy but not look too foolish! But children show their unique personalities early and deserve respect, validation, and trust. This builds a strong and stable sense of identity.

Adults obviously have a lot of power over children including the power of knowing how the world works and how to do things. Adults need to respect a child's valid ignorance and help them learn to succeed in small and large tasks without calling attention to that ignorance in a derogatory way. This requires patience, support, and praise. Children can lose a sense of confidence and become preoccupied with failure if parents don't tolerate and accept their natural ignorance.

To begin evaluating your experience with this need, take a second to think or journal about the following question: *How do you feel about the level of praise and support you received growing up, and how confident in yourself are you, generally?*

Consider these needs in the context of adolescence, where the scale for autonomy and adult responsibility gets larger. Adolescents face the process of making sense of the adult world and considering their own role in it. They face the imperfections of the adult world and the reality of uncertainty and injustice. They do the psychological work of separating themselves from their parents as they build their own identity, which may mean walking awkwardly ahead of their parents at the mall or dressing in a way their families find outlandish. On a more serious note, adolescents can challenge limits in ways that can be dangerous or self-destructive. Parents have the tough job of being aware of and sometimes tolerating "bad" behavior, allowing their teen to make mistakes and learn from them, while still being a supportive and protective presence in ways that teens, who are after all still young, need them to be. And teens need their parents to know how to skillfully walk that line.

At a deeper level and part of the nexus of individual identity and acceptance in society, children and teens must cope with, and need support with, the challenge of belonging to groups on the receiving end of hatred, prejudice, and systemic discrimination.

At a different scale, even unusual tastes, interests, passions, and ambitions can be a challenge to thrive with, depending on social context.

Take a moment to think or journal about the following question: *What messages did you receive growing up about being confident and having pride in your identity?*

Validated Feelings and Needs

As a child, how much did you feel that it was okay to say how you felt and what you needed? Or to speak up when something wasn't fair, didn't make sense, didn't feel good, or was not what you wanted? How much did you feel entitled to what you wanted? The reality is this is always a negotiation, even with a crying infant. And if a child can't get what they want, they may need some care and consolation for the disappointment. Kids need to know there are people around who have them in mind, who are thinking about their feelings. When adults don't validate a child's desires, even when those desires can't be fulfilled, it can cause lasting hurt.

The sense that you may *deserve* to have your needs met and your feelings respected can be challenging for you, as an adult, to accept, especially if this was never part of your childhood experience. "What's so special about me?" But that's just it. As corny as this may sound, you're special because you're you, and you deserved to feel that way— especially as a child, in the most formative time of life.

The experience of being the center or primary subject of a caregiver's attention is a crucial phase of childhood experience. Obviously, this doesn't continue far into adulthood (unless there's narcissism involved), at which point it becomes equally important to recognize that you and your needs are not the *only* ones that matter, but for a time, this is a key ingredient to developing good self-esteem. Children need to experience a period of time where yes, they are the center of the universe!

How much validation was given to you in childhood? Can you see that the need for validation is a feeling about dignity, not just vanity or entitlement? Can you allow yourself to feel that you deserve love and admiration and that your emotional needs are valid?

Loving Discipline and Limits

Loving discipline is about compassionate limit-setting—limit-setting that involves firmness as well as understanding and flexibility. A key aspect of this need is that it sets up a lifelong dynamic for the child as they grow into adulthood. So often, therapy clients as adults are still coping with that punitive parental voice in their head making them feel unnecessarily badly about themselves. Or people are unable to limit their own impulses because, starting early, they were never taught how to. Children take in discipline as a lesson on how to set their own limits and on what attitude to take in getting what they want or not getting what they want all the time. This certainly resonates into adulthood.

Very often a person's childhood experience of discipline becomes a powerful force in adulthood. There is the obvious example of having a parent who is too permissive or unstructured, leading to poor follow-through or impulsiveness in adulthood. Often people develop an internal conflict around discipline, where one side is overly demanding and punitive and another side is impulsive and rebellious in response, and there is a dramatic flipping between them. Think of the ups and downs that can happen around dieting: an overly spartan diet with no pleasure can lead to acting out in response, with overdoing it on "cheat foods." When there's no middle ground between the two sides, discipline and limit-setting are painful.

How tolerant are you of your mistakes? Do you allow yourself a break? How well can you get through boring tasks and remember that they won't last forever? What was your experience of discipline growing up?

Joy, Playfulness, and Creativity

Think about how good it feels when you're among friends who get your sense of humor. There's a feeling that you are being yourself without thinking about it and being appreciated for it. The creative impulse is inherent to everyone and can be cultivated—or repressed—early. It's about the exciting feeling that you are doing something that comes naturally to you, and it may be fun, it may go somewhere, and it is thrillingly welcome.

Some households, depending on what's happening within the family dynamic, can have a humorless, joyless atmosphere, which stifles joy and feelings, rendering them provocative rather than welcome or shared. This can contribute to a sense of false-self, that you can only feel happiness or spontaneity when alone, that it's somehow inappropriate to feel these things in the presence of others. This stifling atmosphere can stay with you and become a creative inhibition in adult life.

How much can you tolerate joy, playfulness, and creativity without demeaning them, mocking them, undermining them, or feeling they're not good enough? How much can you celebrate them? How were joy, playful-ness, and creativity treated in your household during your childhood?

One More Thing

As we reflected on these five core emotional needs and your own childhood experience, was there any aspect of need you experienced that we didn't cover? I hope you're feeling we hit all the important notes. But if we didn't, be sure to journal a bit on other needs you might've felt as a child that went unmet by those who cared for you and validate them.

Core Emotional Needs Outside the Family

There's also a social dimension to core emotional needs that can't be overlooked (as much as mental health professionals can be inclined to). What kind of environment was outside the home, in the neighborhood, in school, and in the community? Are there elements of structural vio-lence, such as racism, white supremacy, homophobia, or ableism that you or your family contended with? Are poverty or other forms of hard-ship factors that affected self-esteem and coherence in the communities you were part of? Was there regular crime or violence in the community that you and your family were exposed to when you were a child? Were there environmental issues, such as pollution leading to learning or health disorders? How were the local schools, health care facilities, and libraries? How much access to good employment was there? All of these social conditions have an impact on your individual experience of core emotional needs and the freedom you might've felt to express the needs you had, to have them validated, to feel dignity and not degradation, and to not feel invisible.

Take a moment to journal about this. *What social factors may have played a role in your experience of yourself and your needs?*

Exercise: Getting to Know "Little You," Part 2

I hope, as you read the previous sections, part of you was reflecting on your own childhood experience of core emotional needs. Now is your chance to get those thoughts on paper. First, using your journal or the "Your Core Needs" worksheet available at http://www.newharbinger.com/50997, answer the questions below to build on the responses you recorded earlier in "Getting to Know Little You, Part 1" by documenting your own unmet core needs—the plot of your childhood experience.

For each of the core emotional needs—safety, love, and care; self-confidence and sense of identity; validated feelings and needs; loving discipline and limits; and joy, playfulness, and creativity—write your responses to the following questions.

1. How was this need met and not met? What is the story of this need in your life, from childhood through adolescence to young adulthood?

2. Regarding this need, do particular memories come to mind or stand out?

3. Do you feel this need is still unmet in your adult life? How do you cope now?

4. How has your temperament played a role in your experience of this need?

5. Does this need feel like a core element of your origin story, a need that says a lot about what's important to you and how you make meaning in life?

In the next part of this exercise, you are going to deepen your relationship with Little You and familiarize yourself with the experience of witnessing your child-self from the perspective of an adult, and not just through your memories.

This is where using your imagination can bring about authentically new experiences of self-awareness. How? We are, of course, accustomed to thinking about our childhood through our own memories because we've always done it that way (naturally). We are holding onto our child perspective even when remembering as an adult. But by imagining yourself as an adult spending time with yourself as a child, you are opening your point of view of your childhood to your adult mind and heart, which allows you to realize and feel things that you can't when you're confined to memories from the time. This is important when trying to understand your unmet core needs.

Now take out your responses to the questions you just answered for each core need and place them next to your childhood photo. You're going to take a second look at the photo, this time through the lens of core needs. Have your journal ready for fresh notes. And this is important: don't review your notes from part 1 just yet.

Now look at the photo of Little You and consider your unmet needs. What thoughts go through your mind as you gaze at yourself and think about unmet needs from your childhood? Write down your thoughts.

Next, look at what you wrote about your unmet needs and your photo (from part 1), and focus on your emotions. What feelings come up for you as you look at Little You now? Write down your feelings.

The following step is important and one of the fundamentals of the schema therapy approach to change: imagine Adult You is meeting Little You. Now that you have an idea of your thoughts and feelings about Little You and unmet needs, how would you relate to Little You as an adult if you both met? Imagine that Adult You is playing the role of parental figure for Little You. How would you try to take care of Little You?

Here, I'm bringing in a key schema therapy experience: imagining your adult-self meeting and caring for your inner child, or Little You:

1. Imagine yourself in a room from the time period of your inner child. Take this slowly and immerse yourself in the experience. What do you see: your bedroom or the family room? What scents are you aware of there? What sounds do you hear? What do you feel on your skin, maybe the flannel of your pajamas or the texture of a rug? Are there toys at your feet? Bring the photo to life and now freeze the image in your mind, like you are pausing a video.

2.   Next, switch your point of view and put yourself in the place of an adult in the room with your inner child. Now, you are playing the ideal-parent role—not how your parents were, but how you feel a parent should be. Remember, you can't change history, but in this moment, as an adult, you can offer your inner child what was needed and missing at the time.

What do you say to your inner child to offer comfort about unmet needs? (Remember to speak in an age-appropriate way.) What would you do with your inner child? Offer a hug? Sit down together to talk? Play a favorite game together?

As you imagine the scene, it may play out in surprising ways, but go with it and take notes about what happens.

3.   Ultimately, the work you do with this image is about really being with your inner child, connecting with all the emotions you might have around those unmet needs, and starting to imagine what it would feel like to get what you need. So, let's explore further. How does your inner child feel after spending some time with Adult You? Note what your inner child feels.

4.   Next, take out your notes from part 1. Place them side-by-side with the notes you just took from part 2. Compare your notes from part 1 and part 2. What changes do you notice in your thoughts and feelings about your inner child from part 1 to part 2? How has your attitude toward your inner child changed after considering your unmet core emotional needs and doing the imagery exercise with them? Note the changes in outlook you've observed.

I am hoping that you did, in fact, see a change from part 1 to part 2 and that you were able to open yourself to more compassion for your inner child. This reaction is not the case for everyone however. You may have noticed some negative or uncomfortable feelings or reactions to Little You and their unmet needs. That's okay. Or you may also notice that you felt nothing for your inner child. That's okay too. These are not uncommon reactions and probably very understandable based on the context you grew up in and your temperament. What's important here is you have met your inner child and a dialogue has begun. This is the key to understanding why you react the way you do, which is the plot of your life.

Once Adult You was able to spend some time with your inner child, I hope you were able to really feel the story of your life in the most fundamental sense. Ultimately, your experience of unmet needs gives depth and meaning to your life, what you value, and what you long for. You responded to these unmet needs with particular ways of coping, which hardened into schemas. Thanks to the investigation you've done in this chapter, you have your origin story, or the plot you keep reliving—the stories you learned to believe your life is about. Next, you'll learn how to break out of these stories, to free your inner child from them, so you can trust Adult You to write new stories and consciously give new meaning to your life based on your values.

Chapter 3

What Are Your Schemas, and Where Do They Come From?

In this chapter, you'll have a chance to review brief "portraits" of all eighteen schemas to see which resonate in your life. I'll help you work out which of your schemas are the most triggering—your core schemas. Then you can try some exercises to help connect with memories or impressions of when these schemas formed in your childhood—or in your origin story, as I like to say. There are some expressive writing exercises later in the chapter to help you understand the situations and relationships that trigger your schemas and the particular ways you think and feel when triggered. This way, you'll be set up to notice when you're triggered—which is one of the biggest challenges to overcoming troublesome coping skills; once you can notice when it's happening, you're more than halfway there.

What Schemas Are

A schema is a snapshot from a moment in time in your childhood when a particular experience was engrained within you as a kind of "rule" explaining how things worked in your world: how your relationships were meant to go and how you should feel about yourself, the people close to you, as well as the world.

It's going to be super important to understand the roots of your schemas, which are found in your origin story. Once you have some insight into the origins of your schemas, you'll have a good analytic perspective on what triggers you now, in your adult life. You will then have a compassionate understanding of what you were coping with as a child, what you needed, and what would have helped. This will point the way to helping you provide for yourself now.

Schema Portraits

I explain each schema portrait from three perspectives to help you figure out which schemas play strong roles in your life: how the schema may sound in your head, how it may affect your daily life now, and how your childhood experience may have formed the schema. Here's how they're arranged along with the questions to ask yourself to determine the role (if any) the schema plays in your life now:

- **Voice:** Do your inner thoughts sound like this?

- **In daily life:** Does the schema play out in your daily life this way?

- **Childhood experience:** Does your childhood experience sound like this?

As you read through the schemas, see which ones feel like they apply to you. You should expect a couple of them to resonate, if not more. Some folks connect with just one or two schemas; others relate to a lot of them. If you end up with several schemas, you may feel concerned: "Does this mean I'm in bad shape?" The truth is that having a lot of schemas may well indicate you face formidable life challenges, but it doesn't necessarily mean your challenges are debilitating. At the end of the day, it's up to you to decide how you're doing with life's challenges and whether you may need the help of a professional to cope. But it's okay—people can have a lot of schemas and lead a successful, fulfilling life.

Emotional Deprivation

Voice. "I'm hurting emotionally, and I'm disappointed that you aren't seeing that. I may give you another chance to see that I need your affection, but let's face it, you'll probably let me down. It feels like people usually let me down. Sometimes I lose my temper, and the resentment comes out."

In daily life. There is a paradox to this schema in the way it might manifest in your daily life. You may feel used to getting by without a lot of affection, but this also upsets you. You may even come across as emotionally cool, but this is only because you've adjusted to the idea that you live in a world where people don't respect your feelings. If you have this schema, you may be so used to feeling emotionally deprived that you expect deprivation even when it's not happening. This leaves you feeling perpetually resentful. There are times when you express anger with a loved one for being neglectful, and it shocks them. "What did I do wrong?!" And they may point out times when they are affectionate, but you don't see it.

Childhood experience. If your parents were not emotionally attuned, they might've done a good job providing physical care for you, but not emotional attunement—the ability to sense or appropriately respond to your emotional states. If your parents were uncomfortable with emotion and didn't provide a lot of affection, you could have been left feeling hurt, angry, and resentful. And you may have given up trying to get attention, thinking *What's the point?* but still hurting about it.

Abandonment

Voice. "I'm so afraid of being abandoned that I think about it too much. All I know is, it feels like being lost, afraid, lonely, and helpless."

In daily life. Abandonment schema is profound and intense. It may be underlying other schemas, so at first, it may be hard to see because it feels so close. For example, you may feel panic and fear about loss during an argument with someone close and rush to say or do whatever you must to stop the argument or please the other person.

Childhood experience. If, as an infant or a child, you couldn't count on your caregivers to be there for you, you may have had the experience of feeling at risk and fear being abandoned all the time—as if it were life or death. Experiences of abandonment can be traumatic for a child, especially if the child doesn't have a solid base of trust in a caregiver. If you have had experiences like this as a child or feel these intense fears are in your attachment patterns now, this may be your schema.

Mistrust or Abuse

Voice. "I need to be careful because the world is a mean and dangerous place. People will hurt me. People are mean and cruel, even if they don't know it, and that's just a fact I need to get used to."

In daily life. Those of us with the mistrust or abuse schema have been hurt in the past, and we may come to believe that we should expect people will hurt us. It may sound like a paradox, but if you have this schema, you may be more tolerant of being treated poorly than you should, just because it's a familiar situation for you. When you get out of a bad relationship, you may find yourself asking, "Why did I put up with that for so long?" On the flipside, you may be avoidant of intimacy because you don't want to get burned.

Childhood experience. This set of feelings commonly comes from growing up in an openly abusive household, whether emotional, physical, sexual, or all the above. Being bullied as a youth or adolescent is also a huge factor in mistrust or abuse.

Social Isolation

Voice. "I really can't be myself unless I'm alone. It's so much work being around others; it's like the pressure is always on; I can't relax. People are draining to be around, they take advantage of me, or I just don't relate, and it is so much easier being alone."

In daily life. If you have social isolation schema, you likely find it difficult to feel and be authentic with others, and it's a lot of work. You may have a sense that you need your batteries charged when you're alone to make up for how draining it can be to be "on" around other people. Socially, you may believe you're a misfit by nature because others seem to be more comfortable being social than you are.

Childhood experience. Social isolation schema comes from a scenario where a child is made to feel that they can't be themselves, that they must follow strict rules. Or they learn that certain natural behaviors are unacceptable, that there is something wrong with being authentic, or that being authentic will be punished or judged. When this happens to you, you may end up gravitating toward your own private world as a means of recovering from the fatigue of performing. Being alone is safe.

Defectiveness

Voice. "I can't let people get close to the real me because if they do, they will reject me. I don't even know why people don't reject me anyway. I feel like I can't date anyone because I'm not good enough. For these reasons, I don't let anyone get close. I have to hide who I really am because I'm just wrong, bad, fucked up, hopeless."

In daily life. You may feel convinced that you're so flawed that you must hide your true self. Whether it's a specific personality trait, your appearance or body, your past, or other issues, the defectiveness makes you feel totally unacceptable.

Childhood experience. Defectiveness schema comes not just from parent or caregiver neglect, but also from the derisive, critical, or even disgusted tone caregivers can take with a child. It's hard to overemphasize how destructive to self-esteem a caregiver's tone can be, particularly when it's disgust. Children are highly tuned in to tone and take it very hard. A tone of disgust translates directly to children feeling they are defective. "There must be something wrong with me that is beyond my power to change."

Failure

Voice. "I really can't accomplish anything I set out to do. It's a miracle I've gotten this far in life without anyone seeing through me. I will not put myself out there and try because I know I will fail, so what's the point? I've never been very good and always screw things up, even since I was a kid. I usually feel imposter syndrome and have a really hard time believing I have done anything well."

In daily life. If you have failure schema—since you're convinced you can never accomplish things—you might engage in a lot of avoidance of work you have to do, especially procrastination. It's like you're putting off the terrible experience of failure you feel will inevitably come with anything you try, so you may wait until you have no choice but to do the work.

Childhood experience. Parents can become invested in teaching their children how to do things in a punitive way, which implies the child is failing. It's not hard to picture. Adults often have little patience for the ignorance or naivete that naturally comes with being a child and can hold children's inexperience against them. Parents like this see helping their kid as a chore, and it's clear in their tone. Your parent may even have believed they were helping you by using a harsh, impatient, punitive tone—trying to toughen you up—but it can leave you believing there must be something about you that fails.

Dependence

Voice. "I really don't do well taking initiative on anything; I believe I'm better off just relying on others; that's who I am. I really need people in my life to help me run things. I'm also very afraid that if the people I depend on abandon me, I won't be able to take care of myself. It's scary!"

In daily life. People with dependence schema hold on very tightly to others and rely on them too much for guidance. Dependence can strain your relationships, as people with dependence schema can resent others for the control they have, and friends and sometimes family resent the dependence. At work, dependence schema can translate as lack of initiative and become an obstacle to advancement and success, leaving you in support roles in the background.

Childhood experience. Dependence schema comes out of a dynamic where a caregiver has poor boundaries with the child and is overly involved, preventing the child from trying and failing with the normal life activities involved in the process of growing up.

Vulnerability

Voice. "Life is full of risks and potential pain and loss. I spend a lot of time worrying and protecting myself. I think of the worst-case scenarios so I can be prepared. I can picture really terrible things happening to me if I let my mind wander."

In daily life. You may feel held back by the fear of an overwhelming thing happening. You may worry of personally feeling overwhelmed in a situation or some hurtful or dangerous thing befalling you—a misfortune, accident, unlucky harm. The worry can be oppressive and very often take up a lot of space in your life. Obviously, this schema can be tricky, because if you are living in a risky scenario, such as dealing with racism and structural violence, it's healthy to be aware of vulnerability. With the climate crisis, it may be unrealistic to deny risk from natural catastrophes and ultimately global vulnerability.

Childhood experience. This schema is born out of an experience of vulnerability and instability in childhood, which left a lasting fear. It's important to understand how deeply feelings of vulnerability can run. To really get it, put yourself in the shoes of a child. You are utterly dependent on adult caregivers for a sense of security and safety and to lose that sense of safety is a feeling of utter loss, danger, panic, insecurity, and emptiness.

Enmeshment

Voice. "I am always worrying about my family or my partner. I get really caught up in other people's feelings, what they are going through, and what they need. I think about other people more than myself. I feel so tied to other people that my own sense of self is linked with them, and I find my self-esteem from being together."

In daily life. Of course, we all need others for support, community, and love, and part of self-care is providing ourselves with fulfilling relationships. But at the core, we are still in charge of making all this happen—tending to both the relationships we form and the maintenance of our own integrity as individual selves. You may have trouble with this if your family enmeshment experience still feels strong and necessary. Do you have trouble standing by your own opinions and preferences? Is it hard to be assertive about what you need? Does the idea of being independent make you feel empty or guilty?

Childhood experience. Some families are so close that they become like one psychological unit. During child development, parents can enmesh with their children as a way to bolster their own self-esteem. As a result, the family does everything together, and family members feel like they can't make decisions without the others' opinion.

Subjugation

Voice. "I find myself always going along with what other people say, want, or need. I feel like I have to keep everyone else happy, which usually means going along with them. It has always felt like it has to be this way. Sometimes it makes me angry, though usually I just hold in my anger. I might even visualize getting angry with someone and what I would say, but I never do it."

In daily life. You tend to give in or go along with others, even when they don't ask you to. You have a strong gut feeling that this is how you have to be in relationships. The flip side is that subjugation schema tends to make everyone involved frustrated and angry sooner or later. People with the schema get angry with themselves for giving in or with others for supposedly making them do it.

Childhood experience. Subjugation schema comes from problematic boundaries between child and caregiver, which involve a devaluing of the child's needs and priorities in the face of the caregiver's. Caregivers may be abusive, narcissistic, or simply preoccupied with their own needs. It can painfully feel like taking care of others is the price of entry into this life and as if it will only hurt to challenge that rule.

Self-Sacrifice

Voice. "I am always ready to put myself out there and volunteer, help someone else, or get involved. I just want to help, and people appreciate it. I also feel like I have to take care of other people in order for them to want me. I feel like I'm not good enough, and I have to prove myself or sacrifice and work for love and acceptance. If I say what I need, I usually feel guilty or like I'm asking for too much."

In daily life. The way self-sacrifice schema manifests is different from subjugation schema; self-sacrifice is not about giving in to the will of others, but about always voluntarily sacrificing oneself for others to one's own detriment. If you have this schema, you may even find you are making sacrifices for people you wish you wouldn't, but it feels like it's the right thing to do.

Childhood experience. Self-sacrifice schema comes from a childhood dynamic where the child is in a position of worrying that they are too much of a burden for the caregiver.

Emotional Inhibition

Voice. "I don't really need to say anything! There's no problem here, I've reviewed everything rationally, and I understand what is happening, so there's no need to have any feelings about it. Sometimes people say to me something like, 'Why aren't you angry about this?' or 'Wow, this must be upsetting,' and I don't understand why they bother. It makes me feel awkward to have someone focus on what I should be feeling."

In daily life. You may get through your day without having many feelings. You may not even know you're filtering out your feelings because it's been happening so long. If you cut emotion out, you may have trouble seeing how it impacts your quality of life. It's hard to tell what you need. Playfulness and joy may be absent. You may come across as cold to others.

Childhood experience. People with this schema are raised in a situation where expressing emotion may cause trouble or punishment. There are very often cultural or generational factors involved in this schema, where parents were raised with the "children should be seen and not heard" belief and enforce it with their own children.

Unrelenting Standards

Voice. "I am constantly worrying about doing a good job, and if there is any sign that I have not done the best and better than everyone else, I feel inconsolable and tell myself I must work even harder. I usually have "Sunday scaries" and feel anxiety about returning to work Monday. At the end of the day, it works out because if I didn't have this attitude, I would not have gotten as far as I have in life."

In daily life. If you have unrelenting standards schema, you are often a high achiever (workaholic?) who feels like you've done enough only when you are completely exhausted and worked long hours. You may have a hard time accepting praise or compliments, always feeling like you're falling short. You feel insecurity or imposter syndrome, always believing you are underperforming or could do better. You tend to turn everything, even leisure activities, into a kind of work. You may even judge yourself harshly about your performance in therapy!

Childhood experience. This is another schema that often comes from a childhood context in which caregivers didn't really respect a child's limitations or pushed the child to perform beyond what's reasonable. Very often a parent believes they are helping a child by being demanding and punitive with them to improve their skills and performance.

Guarded, Entitled, or Grandiose

Voice. "My point of view is so urgent to me that I need to make sure you know what it is, and I am so focused on it that I'm not thinking about anything else. It's only fair! Or I may need to hold my own point of view because it feels more secure that way—other people are invasive. I need to push myself hard for people to hear and consider me. On the other hand, I may be so accustomed to getting my way that I don't really consider what other people think. Why should I? If I'm already getting what I need—or if I don't even really need other people—then why should I bother? Not my problem. I may spend the entire time in a conversation talking about myself without asking the other person what they think. I'll get to what you think in a minute."

In daily life. You may feel you really need to express yourself, as though it's particularly important for all involved that your ideas be aired. You may notice that you often end up neglecting others' points of view or needs in the way you speak to them or behave with them. You may also tend to respond aggressively when you're challenged. You may think the rules don't apply to you, that you're special. On the other hand, you may feel burdened by your lot in life, that you are put out by your life. However, you are still mostly only thinking about yourself and your difficulty. You may also feel that you have to hold on to your own point of view and defend it against all others. You can't afford to let other people's opinion threaten your own.

Childhood experience. This schema often involves extremes in a childhood experience. For example, overattentive and protective caregivers leave a child believing their needs should always be attended to by others. Or a child experiences a caregiver who personally has a difficult personality that is too much for the child to bear, and this schema becomes a wall to protect the child from being overwhelmed by their caregiver.

Insufficient Self-Control

Voice. "Fuck it, I'm tired of having to do all this work, make all this sacrifice, or deal with all this noise. I need a break, and I'm going to do what I want. I just want to be me, and that means enjoying myself now and not worrying about all the pressure I'm under. I don't want to think about all that hard stuff, and there's nothing wrong with taking a break. I deserve it. And if I'm pushed too hard, this is my response: I don't give a shit right now. I'm doing what I want! How do you like me now?!"

In daily life. In the substance-abuse recovery community, people say they "got a case of the fuck-its." That applies here. This schema is a resistance that often looks like procrastination, the detachment of too much screen time, having a hard time getting out of bed, substance abuse, or just avoiding work in ways that cause problems. This schema can make you feel split. You may know you need to work out, not drink that sugar soda, or not have that pork bun, but you can't stop yourself or may only feel regret later. This schema can become quite a problem, threatening your performance at work or your ability to succeed with other personal life goals.

Childhood experience. This is another schema with a paradox. It may come from having either too lenient an upbringing or one that was too strict. As you got older and faced more consequences for your schema (such as trouble in school or doing chores), any punishment (or negligence) you faced may have reinforced your rebellious reaction.

Approval Seeking

Voice. "I know I may ask you this a lot, but is everything okay? Are we okay? I hope you're happy with me and how things are going, and yes, I know I ask you that a lot. A lot of what I do is based on whether I'm getting someone's attention and approval. I really need it. And I never really catch up on the attention, so I hang on to my boss's words and do whatever she wants; that's super important."

In daily life. This approach can be limiting in terms of career, since people with this schema feel like they only exist in the eyes of others. If you have this schema, people may feel, in both work and personal contexts, that they don't "know the real you." Their approval feels like fulfillment.

Childhood experience. Children who develop the approval-seeking schema feel unsettled in themselves or insecure and need the reassurance of approval from parents. This may be because parents were intrusive and overbearing or only showed attention when the child "deserved it." This made love very transactional: unless you're doing something to warrant love and attention, you may not have gotten it.

Negativity or Pessimism

Voice. "Let's face it, I know things just never work out the way I want. It's always been like that, and I see no evidence that things will get better. It may be better for other people, but not for me. I hate it when loved ones tell me to be more positive or that things will get better. They sound stupid when they spout all that positivity. At least I'm smart enough to know the reality, which is that things never work out, and it's better to accept that, so I don't keep getting disappointed. So I'm just going to do what I can to get by, and I'm not going to have big expectations; those are for suckers. I focus on the hard facts."

In daily life. You may hold on to negativity as a way of protecting yourself from the pain of a difficult life. Sound like a paradox? You may tell yourself that if you accept a pessimistic outlook, you'll be less disappointed by dashed hopes and therefore experience less pain. If you don't expect good things to happen, you don't have to worry about being let down. Of course, the problem with this schema is that it is a self-fulfilling prophecy: by avoiding hope, you also cut off the opportunity to make your life better or to allow good things to happen to you. In this way, you can start to pile up proof that you are right to be pessimistic: "After all, when have things ever gone well for me?"

Childhood experience. People with negativity or pessimism schema are often raised by parents with the same schema, who transfer it via their own care for the child. It's also not uncommon to see this schema among people who have suffered widescale upheaval, hardship, or trauma, such as refugees or people who struggled through terrible economic events like the Great Depression. Children who develop negativity or pessimism have often had to live through some ongoing misfortune, such as abuse or neglect at home or bullying at school. The negativity becomes a comfort zone and a way of coping but also a wall against letting people show care and affection.

Punitiveness

Voice. "I'm such an idiot. Why did I make that mistake? I keep fucking things up, and it's unacceptable. Will I ever get my shit together, or am I doomed to be in this bad job or bad relationship forever?"

In daily life. This schema feels like a very private internal voice, and it's one of the loudest schema voices and one of the most challenging to overcome. Your colleagues and loved ones may hear this voice slip out now and then, but you often hear it in harsh internal judgments about yourself and sometimes others.

Childhood experience. Children are powerfully influenced and marked by their parents' disciplinary style. There is an unfortunate streak of sadism in some parenting. A key point on punitiveness, though, is that whatever tone a parent uses is magnified by the child's psyche and then turned inward (barring outright abusive parenting). So however harsh a parent is with the child, the child becomes even harsher with themselves. Punitiveness still has at its core the promise of self-care. "If I were just mean enough to myself, I would really learn the lesson and do better."

All right, those are the eighteen schemas and what they can sound like in your thoughts and look like in your day-to-day life. You also learned a bit about the childhood experiences and child-caregiver dynamics that can lead to the formation of each schema. Could you see different schemas at work in your life as you read? Which of the schemas really struck a chord for you?

Three Priority Schemas for Change

Can I take a moment to check in with you? How did it go reading about those schemas? Some folks are more matter-of-fact about it, while for others, it can be odd and even hard to read about yourself through this lens. Some people find it freeing, like learning about yourself, while others can feel shame, like they are faulty or labeled. Another way to put it is, people have their schemas triggered by reading about their schemas. It's a totally normal part of the process. If it was not hard for you, I hope you're more motivated to learn how to use this insight to transform your coping skills. If it was hard for you, keep in mind that the next steps are intended give you tools to feel better and make change.

As you read the schema portraits, you may have identified as many as three schemas that manifest in your life, or you may have identified more than three. Either way, in this activity, select the three schemas that exert the most influence at this time in your life. Then, for each schema, think about it in ways that are specific to you and your origin story and consider:

- *what it says* (the voice you hear in your head)

- how it *affects your daily life* (your relationships, career, and so on)

- your own *childhood experience* of the schema

- the *emotions* and *body sensations* that accompany this schema.

This is meant to be quick and to the point, so you don't need to put a lot of work into it. Here's an example of a completed response for the unrelenting standards schema:

- What it says: "You're not good enough. You need to excel! That's the only way people will know that you matter. If you don't go above and beyond on this project, you're going to look bad."

- How it affects my daily life: I wake up and feel behind on things every day! I rush to the gym, I feel like I'm not getting far enough in my routine, and from there, everything in my day feels like I'm falling short. Plus, I always work late to make up for it.

- My childhood experience of the schema: My parents really got on me about doing well; they never let up. My dad's tone especially always made me feel like I was just getting by and that I should feel bad.

- The emotions and body sensations that come with this schema: I feel pressure in my chest, like a kind of light anxiety, and it's there with me all the time. It's that feeling like you're late for an appointment and about to get in trouble. Yeah, I feel that a lot!

For each of your three priority schemas, respond to the four prompts above in your journal or on the downloadable worksheet, "Schema Chart," available at http://www.newharbinger.com/50997. This list of three priority schemas will become your schema chart. Hold on to the chart for future reference.

This activity was meant to give the chance to do some cognitive work with your top three schemas, by writing about them and teasing apart the effects they have on your thoughts and your behaviors. Now we're going to move from cognitive to experiential work, as you work to connect with a specific memory and the emotions that come with it.

Connecting with Important Schema Memories

When you clearly see how your schemas impact your daily life, you can start undoing their influence and power over you. A key tool for doing that is using the emotions you experience in a schema today to find how they are echoed in childhood memories. You will see and feel how these schemas are part of your personal story and not just words and concepts on a page.

As you deepen this link between schema concepts and your own feelings and history, you will be opening up to the experience of you as a child, picturing Child You, empathizing with Child You, and feeling the true depth of your childhood unmet needs. In other words, you'll be connecting with your inner child mode: the versions of your inner child that acutely feel needs and react with certain patterns, such as anger, or fear, or rebellion. Thus far, I have been discussing your inner child—the image and memories you have of yourself as a child—and now I'm adding the idea of "inner child mode." As an adult, you have certain mindsets or moods you switch into, and we call them "modes." It's the same with your inner child, who has certain go-to coping reactions to strife: most often anger, or fear and vulnerability, or rebellion. So, we call it the "inner child mode," and it is really just how Little You reacted to schemas.

It may seem a little weird or even uncomfortable to talk about "connecting with your inner child." But to heal psychological difficulties, you have to go back to their source. So connecting with your inner child mode, the "you" that you were when your needs first went unmet, is your wellspring for change in the present. Soon enough, you will be taking your inner child with you as you lead the life you hope to lead, and the kid's going to love it!

The next exercise combines the technique of expressive writing—which, again, helps people connect with emotions they otherwise leave unexpressed—with a commonly used CBT method called imagery work (Pennebaker and Smyth 2016). It will put you back in touch with your inner child and unmet needs. Simply put, imagery is the practice of calling up in an image in your mind, either of a memory or something you create, and working with the thoughts and feelings that arise in reaction to the image. Basically, you'll be calling up an image of the memory of one of your schemas and using the questions below to guide you in reflecting on the thoughts and feelings that come up. Imagery is powerful in that it feels real and holds your attention (Hackman et al. 2011, 11).

Before we begin, keep in mind that when you're doing any mental health exercise in a self-help context, you should remember some key points about healthy boundaries and self-care.

- Schedule the days on which you'll do the exercise in advance, so you know you will make each day happen and commit to it.

- Choose a time and place to do the exercise when you won't be disturbed.

- Look out for any signs of unexpectedly difficult or even traumatic material and stop the exercise anytime if necessary. If the experience you're having is very intense, consider consulting a professional.

- Make sure to keep your writing process safe and private.

- Have pen and paper or computer ready to go when you sit down to start so you can get straight to writing.

- Allow yourself time after writing is complete to debrief and process any difficult feelings that may arise.

Okay, let's get started.

Exercise: Three Priority Schemas

Over a period of three consecutive days, schedule a minimum of twenty minutes per day to do this exercise. You will work with all three of your priority schemas, one at a time, per day. Look over your schema priority notes or the "Schema Chart" worksheet you just completed.

Review the first schema and the emotions and body sensations you noted connected to it. Now close your eyes, sit back comfortably, take a couple of deep breaths, and focus on the feelings and body sensations associated with the schema based on the schema portraits.

When you start to feel them, keep your eyes closed and think of a childhood memory of a time when you were feeling those same emotions and sensations. Once you have an image of a memory to work with, stay in it for enough time for it to stick.

Now open your eyes, and write your answers to the following questions:

- What is happening in this memory?

- What does Child You need in this memory?

- Is Child You getting what they need? If not, why not?

- How is Child You feeling in this memory?

Take a moment to breathe deeply and check in with yourself. How was that to do? How are you feeling now? Your reactions to the exercise may involve some schema triggering, which again, is fine, but may call for a little extra self-care.

Once you have your answers, move on to the next two schemas on your priority chart and repeat with each over the following two days. Once you have completed all three days of exercises, you may find that a lot of memories have been jogged, and you may want to continue journaling on these topics.

You may have found these exercises easy and straight-forward, or you may have been challenged by them. It's okay! We all have different kinds of access to childhood memories, and it's not at all unusual to find that few childhood memories come to mind at all. This is not your fault.

Sometimes our brain makes certain memories harder to access because they're unpleasant or difficult, and sometimes we just haven't been accustomed to calling up memories in the ways this exercise calls for. You can work with a simple image or even a memory fragment if it's connected to your schema feelings.

Another common reaction to this exercise is to be surprised by what memories or thoughts and feelings come up. Again, this is not an unusual reaction, as the more important details of our history can sometimes be scrambled by memory, and looking at our past with fresh, adult eyes is a totally different perspective from the one you grew up with. And that's why this exercise can be so powerful.

Some difficult and painful memories may have come back up too. Remember it's important to touch this first baseline of your triggering emotions and link them to your past. This is just the first step, and you are cultivating how you can validate and care for these feelings. I'm not overlooking that right now may be the first time in your life that you're being there for these feelings.

What's Next?

In this chapter, you got to see what schemas look and feel like in your life. You also made a crucial connection between the schemas you experience in your daily life now and their roots in your childhood. This is the hallmark of the schema therapy approach to deep change: understanding when Child You is triggered and understanding that when Child You is triggered, intense childlike feelings and thoughts can be triggered, which in turn influence your behavior and ways of coping in the present.

So, the next task is to learn to *change* your triggered reactions and maladaptive coping skills, which takes us to learning how schemas influence our behavior. That behavior response is called the "mode," which I'll get into in the next chapter.

You can think of the schemas you uncovered in this chapter as the primary colors of your experience (deep emotional reactions), while modes are the more complicated patterns of behavior made up of combinations of those colors. Next, you'll learn how to read these pictures and change them.

Chapter 4

Modes: The Characters in Your Origin Story

Now that you know your schemas and unmet core emotional needs, you know what triggers your strongest feelings, fears, insecurities, and psychological pain. In this chapter, you're going to learn how these triggers and feelings play out in your life as they influence your mindset and behavior—in other words, how your past affects your present. We are getting to your problematic coping skills and to the particular mindsets that contribute to those problematic coping skills. To keep with the metaphor I introduced last chapter, this chapter is about the characters in your story—known in schema therapy as "modes."

Our mind is impressionable, and during childhood, our experiences with ourselves and others etch into our brains as archetypes that work like semipermanent patterns we see in the world and in the present (schemas, right?). When we recognize those patterns, we switch into a *mindset*. We all operate with several different mindsets, which are modes, almost like characters that we can become as we define and make sense of our experience.

Once you discover how schemas cause modes and learn about the five basic types of modes and their variations, you'll try some exercises to help you understand the modes and identify which modes you have.

By the end of this chapter, you'll have a mode map to compliment your schema chart and an incredibly powerful set of tools to use in the chapters to come.

Is It a Schema or a Mode?

I'd like to set the table for our mode discussion with a simple definition: the term "mode" is a label for a self-state made up of a particular mindset triggered by schemas. That's it. To put it another way, a schema is a simple train of thought or thought pattern, while a mode is more like listening to a real person's complex thoughts and intentions. Schemas feel one-dimensional, while modes feel three-dimensional. Hearing someone express their schema thoughts is a bit like hearing someone explain a rule or a formula: "You must work harder!" "You can't say what you need because it's not important!" Hearing someone express mode experience is like having a full conversation with a character who has a point of view and wants to do something about it: "You were barely able to keep it together in that Zoom meeting yesterday. You really do suck at your job; I can't believe they haven't fired you yet! If you're smart, you should just work hard and keep your head down and not talk."

You can't talk to a schema so much, but you can definitely have a relationship with a mode.

Especially complex or challenging modes are a kind of pod of schemas—that is, you move from simple, triggered feelings and trains of thought (schema) into full moods, behaviors, mindsets, and several schemas at once (a mode). In other words, "schemas are traits, and modes are states" (Young et al. 2003, 41). Schemas are trait-like; they are triggers or reactions much more ingrained in our personality, having formed in our brain as we adapted to our environment and its challenges. Modes are states, or mindsets, we can get into in response both to internal triggering and to our environment, as a means of reacting and coping. The modes I will mostly be discussing here reveal themselves as the coping skills reacting to schemas, which end up causing us so much frustration.

How Mode Awareness Helps You Change

Ultimately, modes fall into five distinct types: the inner child mode, the coping child mode, the difficult coping mode, the inner critic mode, and the healthy caring adult mode. (There are subcategories of modes, which we'll get into later.) These five mode types interact around schema triggering. Here's what the triggering looks like. First, the inner child mode feels unmet needs, which trigger our schemas. In response to these schemas, the coping child, the difficult coping, and the inner critic modes flip on as ways we use to cope. So, while schemas are triggered in the inner child, they appear in the guise of how we cope with them: our coping child, difficult coping, and inner critic modes. The healthy caring adult mode is our ideal mindset, separate from the schema-based (problematic) modes: difficult coping, coping child, and inner critic modes. Schema therapy is about the healthy caring adult mode caring for the needs of the inner child, ideally as a replacement for the problematic modes. Our goal is to get you to a place where your healthy caring adult mode can attend to triggered schemas in ways that are caring rather than problematic for you. So, with your healthy caring adult mode, you may still experience a triggered schema, but you cope in a healthy way, caring for your inner child.

As I'll get to, our healthy caring adult mode will learn to watch over and care for all the modes, with the goal of reducing the action of problematic ones. As part of the therapy process, schema therapists help a client identify their healthy mindset, the person they want to be, so that, when in a dysfunctional mode, the client has a point of reference: "What would a healthy version of me say right now?" That "healthy version of me" is called the "healthy caring adult mode."

I'll be translating this picture into a map soon enough, and in the next section, I will go into each mode in detail with a table to illustrate. But for now, it's important to know that the coping child, difficult coping, and inner critic modes are made up of schemas. Think of these modes as parts of the self, each defined by your schemas.

Modes and Their Schemas

In the table below, the "Mode" column lists the mode categories along with their subcategories. The inner child mode and the healthy caring adult mode are not included, as they are not schema-based. This table matches modes with the schemas commonly associated with them.

Mode	Schemas
Coping child • Vulnerable child • Angry child • Impulsive child • Undisciplined/rebellious child	Emotional deprivation Abandonment Mistrust or abuse Defectiveness Failure Vulnerability Insufficient self-control Dependence
Difficult coping • Compliant surrenderer • Detached protector • Detached self-soother • Self-aggrandizer • Bully	Enmeshment Approval seeking Self-sacrifice Subjugation Emotional inhibition· Social isolation Guarded, entitled, or grandiose

Mode	Schemas
Inner critic	Punitiveness
• Punitive aspect	Negativity or pessimism
• Demanding aspect	Unrelenting standards

Once you are aware of your schemas, you can observe how they influence your behavior, which in turn helps you understand which of your modes is triggered at any given time. And with practice, you will learn to notice your triggered mode *while* it is triggered. Then you can start to develop enough distance from a mode to be free to react differently. You'll be ready to make more informed and self-aware choices about how you react and how you live. This is the core of change in this model.

In this chapter, you'll explore and identify your modes so you can start to interact with them to make change. Just like studying characters in a novel or movie, you will discover the origin and motivations of each of your modes. In your origin story, when you were a child first experiencing schemas, your modes formed as a way of surviving. As you aged and went through different phases of development, these modes became more engrained and automatic. So now, getting to know your modes will help you relate to each of them as if they were real people, who you've known all your life, who were just responding to life's difficulties the only way they knew how. It will be up to you to talk back to these modes and explain to them that things have changed, childhood is over, and there are better ways to handle stress now.

The Five Basic Mode Types

Remember, to understand mode types, you can think of them as the result of your experiences of being imprinted with certain life experiences and of doing your best to make sense of those experiences, work with them, and cope with what life was throwing at you.

Inner Child Mode

The inner child mode is the wellspring of our core emotions, such as sadness, fear, anger, and shame, as well as joy, playfulness, creativity, and need for love. These are all core emotions with a deep need for validation and expression. You already know all about your inner child after chapter 2 and the photo exercises you did with Little You (not to mention the other modes that came up as you looked at the photo). We have a child mode—or inner child—and when things are going well for us, Adult You connects with the deep core emotions in the inner child, and you're okay with validating and attending to those feelings. In other words, the healthy caring adult is connected to the inner child mode: all is well, they are in sync. The trouble starts with the next three mode categories.

Coping Child Mode

The coping child mode reacts in helpless, defensive, or protective ways to the core pain coming out of unmet needs and schemas. Think of a real child reacting to their own pain or discomfort or mistreatment (however they do), and that's this mode. Whenever you encounter your coping child mode, you should ask, "What pain or unmet need is behind this reaction?" You will see your inner child underneath. You will usually experience variations on the coping child mode and get to know a couple versions that come up for you regularly, which I list here as subcategories.

The coping child mode subcategories include:

- vulnerable child

- angry child

- impulsive child

- undisciplined/rebellious child.

For a lot of us, there's definitely a vulnerable child and very often an angry child or an undisciplined child. You can also expand this to picture an angry or rebellious adolescent. So you may have more specific names for your coping child modes based on your own childhood experience. For instance, you may relate more to abandoned child, neglected child, lonely child, or abused child. But whatever you prefer to call yours, the core mode concept is we all have a coping child mode at heart.

Difficult Coping Mode

One way to think of the difficult coping mode is as the unique developments of a person's temperament and life circumstances coming together in the form of a survival pattern.

The difficult coping mode subcategories include:

- compliant surrenderer

- detached protector

- detached self-soother

- self-aggrandizer

- bully.

The coping modes often start to form just prior to the "tween" age window, set in, and stay with us into adulthood.

Inner Critic Mode

Just as the inner child mode is a time capsule of child self-states, the inner critic mode is a time capsule of the child's experience of discipline and authority. Generally, there are two subcategories to the inner critic mode: the demanding aspect and the punitive aspect. You might experience an inner critic that's more one aspect or the other or a blend of both. As with the coping child mode, feel free to name your own inner critic in a way that feels more authentic. You may call yours "the Taskmaster," or "Ms. Perfect." But remember, for you "results may vary," and it's important to have a name for your inner critic that feels real.

The inner critic mode is especially difficult to manage due to the unreasonable demands or criticism it burdens you with, leading to problems with self-esteem and self-confidence.

The inner critic mode is quite common—everyone has one. It damages self-esteem, often causing depression and anxiety, and can drive people to therapy. The inner critic can be deeply engrained and a challenge to overcome. You may think it obvious that if you have a demanding, irrational bully in your head, you would naturally want it out. The thing is, the inner critic mode holds the kind of authority a parent holds over a dependent child, making you want to trust them and to believe that they see reality more clearly than you and that they are looking out for your best interests. You likely have a history with your inner critic: you can point to times in the past when it helped you succeed. The challenge with overcoming the inner critic is to prove to yourself that you can care for yourself, be safe, and have ambitions without being mean to yourself or irrationally demanding.

Healthy Caring Adult Mode

The healthy caring adult mode is characterized by mindsets and ways of behaving that are connected to positive feelings, generative thoughts, and motivations that help you feel effective in the world, fulfilled, and emotionally aware.

The goal of this book—and schema therapy—is to help you access, develop, and live in your healthy caring adult mode so you can get past all the problematic modes and connect with your inner child. This is how you validate, experience, and express the richness of your core emotions. The final two chapters of this book are devoted entirely to those goals. For now, think of the healthy caring adult as your compassionate, well-grounded self, a place from which you can manage your other modes, connect with your inner child, and make real improvements in your life.

How the Five Mode Types Play Roles in Your Origin Story

Have you ever read the printed version of a stage play? At the beginning, before the dialogue and action of the play starts, you'll see a list of the characters. Essentially, what you just read above is the list of characters making up the play of your personality. You have a list of the characters in the story (modes) and may have come up with your own special names for your characters. So now the question is, how do your characters fit into your origin story as we explored it in chapter 2? Your origin story was about Little You's core emotional needs, how they were met and unmet in your family, and why. We're going to give the mode characters in your play a plot and backstory, based on your childhood origin story.

Let's take another look at your mode types, this time as part of your origin story:

Mode	Role in Origin Story
Inner child	Your inner child, who wants to play, learn, grow, and be loved, is entitled to a full range of healthy emotions. "I have needs, will you help?"
Coping child	When needs are unmet, the child may get angry, or hopeless and hurt, or act out and resist. "I NEED YOU, I'M ANGRY, I'M SCARED!"

Mode	Role in Origin Story
Difficult coping	The alternate versions of adolescent or Adult You want to avoid, ignore, or forget your inner child—too much trouble! "It's best to pretend that child isn't here!"
Inner critic	The punitive and demanding Adult You thinks the best form of care is being mean and demanding. "This child is pathetic, lazy, or just not good enough; they should do more!"
Healthy caring adult	The caring adult soothes and protects your inner child, manages well-being, motivation, assertiveness, creativity, and adaptability. "I'm going to deal with all of these modes coming between my inner child and me, so I can take care."

The plot of the story is this: There is a young child who has needs, like everyone does. But they go unmet, and now the child is having to cope. Around the child, pop up a row of coping versions of itself: one in pain, one being neglected, one crying for help and love, one lashing out in anger, and one trying to hide in the corner. These kids are surrounded by a row of adults who aren't good at caring for or comforting the child: they avoid the child, just accept the child is hurting, or act intolerant and critical of the child for being needy. And none of these adults is able to be present with the child's tough feelings, validate them, and love the child—the one thing the child needs most. And then there's your healthy caring adult, who is going to reach the inner child and care for their needs so the other modes aren't necessary.

While each of us has a story that looks unique, the elements I laid out here are the key structure of the story we all share. With your own particular characters and a unique tone to the plot; you can relate the details of your own origin story to this general framework.

By now you are probably itching to try this model out, so let's get going!

Mode Portraits

Just like the schema portraits in the last chapter, you're going to take the same approach identify your likely modes. Once you have an idea of which modes you connect to, you'll plot them on a chart. After that, there's a fun exercise to help you visualize your modes as a map so you can better work with them.

First, I'm going to describe the three types of modes that can cause difficulty for you. Remember, the first mode is the inner child mode, and the fifth mode is the healthy caring adult, and future chapters will be devoted to how they connect. Similar to the schemas in the last chapter, I explain each mode portrait from the perspectives of your thoughts and behavior:

- **Voice:** Do your inner thoughts sound like this?

- **In daily life:** Does the mode play out in your daily behavior this way?

Inner Child Mode

Voice. "I just want to do my thing! I go with whatever I'm feeling: if I'm sad, I act sad; if I'm happy, I show it; if I want to play, I start playing right here; if I want affection, I'll tell you; if I'm tired, I want to sleep. I feel what I feel, and I want to act on what I feel. There's nothing wrong with that, I deserve it like all kids do!"

In daily life. Whenever you feel fulfilled or self-actualized—connected with what you're feeling and acting on it—there is an unbroken line of communication with your inner child mode. This may include the full range of feelings ranging from sad and hurt to joyous and silly. If you're feeling it and expressing it, you're connected with your inner child.

Coping Child Mode

Voice. "I'm angry, and I don't care. Everybody lets me down. I'm doing this, and you can't stop me. I'm fine alone; I don't need anyone. I just don't give a shit; I'm not doing it. I'm so angry I want to explode! I'm just vibing. Can't I relax without being bothered? It's unfair I have to do this."

You might also hear, "I'm scared and feel helpless!" or "I'm just going to be alone and away from everyone!" or "I'm so ashamed, I guess I'm unlovable." Also, very importantly, just as sometimes children can't put their needs into words, you may notice intense moods or states of emptiness, which you can imagine as a child in pain without the words to use.

In daily life. The coping child mode reacts to unmet needs with sadness, anger, or fear. These child reactions disrupt behavior daily life, causing frustration, strife, and stuckness. You may notice impulsiveness, the rumble of intense anger, lack of discipline, or procrastination. You may see this in laziness, acting out, temper tantrums, rebelliousness, isolation, or sulking.

Difficult Coping Mode

The difficult coping mode generally includes five subcategories: the compliant surrenderer, the detached protector, the detached self-soother, the self-aggrandizer, and the bully. What they have in common is that they each react to schemas in ways that perpetuate the schemas, rather than manage them. Chances are you may have one or two diffi-cult coping modes clearly operating as influences in your life.

COMPLIANT SURRENDERER

Voice. "It's really not worth getting upset about. You never know, things could be worse. Don't rock the boat or you'll find yourself in a worse place. This may actually be your fault, and if things get worse, you may not be able to handle it. You should really work on just managing this better and stop complaining. You really don't have a right to complain."

In daily life. You tend to avoid conflict, you may feel people treat you unfairly, but you keep silent and doubt your own feelings. You may even believe you deserve this situation because of your flaws and the idea that you can't make it alone. You find that you tend to be passive, following others' directions and avoiding taking risks. In both career and relationships, you may find you go along with what others want. (And there might be an angry child deep down, hoping to say something about this!)

DETACHED PROTECTOR

Voice. "You do not want to open yourself up to these emotions, it's going to cause a lot of pain, and it won't be worth it. Focus on what you can do now rather than get involved in complicated emotions or the past. You can't change the past, so why bother?"

There is also an angry detached protector: "I just don't want to talk about it! We don't have to get bogged down with feelings; they aren't useful! Let's just talk about something else."

In daily life. People experience you as formal or rigid, or even uptight; it's hard to know what you feel and, as a result, who you are. You certainly have friends and relationships, but you may be a bit of a mystery to others in terms of what you feel. You may get angry or dismissive with people who try to connect with your feelings and that interferes with building strong, long-term relationships.

DETACHED SELF-SOOTHER

Voice. "I just need to chill. Maybe some binge-watching, drinking, or food. Maybe social media or web surfing for hours. Tune out. Thinking about 'real stuff' is really draining. Besides, I'm tired and I need a break! Maybe some other time!"

In daily life. As much as possible, you are distracting yourself, with podcasts at lunch, binge-watching in the evening, video games, sometimes alcohol or drugs, or even reading a lot of nonfiction (fiction has characters who may have feelings!). You may dread evenings, weekends, and holidays for the free time that can be depressing to try to fill. Detaching is like a trap—the more badly you feel, the more you need to detach, but the more you detach, the worse you feel.

SELF-AGGRANDIZER

Voice. "Can I tell you about the cool thing I did this week, and how well I'm doing? I'm really good with things and just want you to know. I don't like to dwell on the negative, especially when I have so many great things going on. Okay, enough talk about me—What do *you* think about me?" The voice can also be aggressive and difficult: "You have no business bothering me about this—I really have better things to do! I shouldn't have to bother with this; it's beneath me. You should treat me with more respect!"

In daily life. You spend a lot of time talking about your accomplishments, being the center of attention, and worrying that you aren't. Keeping the focus on your good points keeps attention away from what you may think are flaws, which are very painful for you. And if you're of the more aggressive type of self-aggrandizer, you may have heard from others that you are a "strong personality" or hard to work with. You may be a less aggressive aggrandizer and seldom crow your own accomplishments, but you remain convinced that you are correct and have the answers.

BULLY

Voice. "I can't believe you would say that about me! I'M NOT AT ALL LIKE THAT, and it's really pathetic that you would even think that, so you must have some kind of problem or maybe you're just not very bright. *I'm* not the only one who calls names; you call me names all the time."

In daily life. Certain sensitive points may trigger you to lose your temper and fiercely attack people. It may be something about your appearance or being criticized. Also, when people tell you something they may need, you hear it as a criticism, get very defensive, and go on the attack. This includes projecting insecurities about your own flaws into attacks on others. Underneath all the sound and fury is an insecure inner child who feels rejected.

Inner Critic Mode

There are two subcategories of the inner critic mode: punitive aspect and demanding aspect.

PUNITIVE ASPECT

Voice. "You're really pathetic. You probably couldn't manage to keep friends even if you made any. You don't know how to talk to people—you always turn people off! So why bother? On the other hand, I can also criticize you for being pathetic and giving up—that is, for listening to me!"

The punitive voice gets you coming and going, attacks you for not doing something, and will also attack you for *doing* it! "There is something really wrong with you, which is causing all your troubles. Stop whining about it."

In daily life. You're harsh with yourself, and even mean—a lot. It feels like if you weren't harsh with yourself, bad things would happen to you, or you would be the bad person you worry deep down you really are. (Of course, deep down, you worry you are a bad person because the inner critic tells you that you are!) You also turn this harsh, judgmental point of view on others at times, usually the ones close to you. You may notice, say, in the shower, that a critical voice is running in your head nonstop, saying mean things about yourself and others.

DEMANDING ASPECT

Voice. "You have not done enough and need to keep working hard on this. Get up earlier; you really don't get to have a break; you need to be the best, or at least catch up, to prove yourself. You don't get a weekend, and if you take time off, I'll make sure you feel guilty about it. You should always be self-deprecating too because you just aren't good enough without working harder than everyone else."

In daily life. You are likely a workaholic and have a hard time relaxing, feeling the need to prove yourself over and over, with a strong belief you have to work harder than everyone else just to break even. The idea of working only as much as anyone else does, or as much as you are asked to, fills you with anxiety that something bad will happen. Boundaries with work are a problem.

Exercise: Identifying Your Modes

In this exercise, you're going to connect to your modes. Over a period of three consecutive days, schedule a minimum of twenty minutes per day to do each segment of this exercise. You may need more or less time, depending on how much comes up for you. Try to stay open-minded about your experience with this exercise; some people have more difficulty than others connecting with their modes, and that's completely okay. Each of the mode types is slightly different, so each segment of this exercise differs too. If you don't feel a strong connection to a particular mode as I describe it, it may not be particularly relevant for you, so you can move on to the next one in the list.

Inner Child Mode

You've already done a lot of work on this mode in chapter 2, with the Little You exercises that were about your inner child. So, you don't absolutely need to put aside writing time for this mode. However, I would like you to think over a couple of questions, and you can, of course, write about them if it's useful. (It never hurts to take an opportunity to nurture your sense of your inner child.) Depending on your childhood experience, some of these questions may be tough, especially if you didn't have a lot of opportunity to have these feelings validated by others. But reflect on how you felt them in whatever setting it was, whether in the family home, in school, with friends, or with good, helpful mentors.

Writing Prompts

- What were your best and most loveable qualities as a child? Describe how you felt joy, playfulness, curiosity, creativity, enthusiasm, love, and freely expressed your needs.

- Describe how you felt and expressed your dependency on others and your need to have affection from others.

- Describe how you still experience the above qualities now, as an adult. You might also describe how Adult You would like to reconnect more with these qualities. This is Adult You wanting to get closer to your inner child. You need each other!

Coping Child Mode

You may not necessarily notice that you have a coping child mode. But first think about the ways a coping child mode can appear, with the most common being vulnerable child, angry child, impulsive child, and undisciplined or rebellious child. Would you say that anger, impulsiveness, being undisciplined, or rebelliousness is a disruptive issue for you in your adult life? If so, I suggest putting aside some time for this segment of the exercise.

You are looking for a link between your mindsets and behaviors now and how they may be rooted in childhood. Consider whether you have variations on these themes in your experience now.

- The *vulnerable child* is triggered by schemas and feelings related to feeling rejected, shamed, flawed, scared, and vulnerable. Make sure your name for this part of you feels like a good fit. Other useful terms may be abandoned child, abused child, or neglected child, depending on your history.

- The *angry child* is triggered by themes such as injustice ("It's not fair!"), neglect ("Pay attention to me!"), or fear and mistrust ("I don't trust you. You hurt me!"). Remember, our adult anger is naturally rooted in our childhood anger. This doesn't necessarily mean that the angry child mode is a problem for

Adult You. Ask yourself these questions: Would you consider anger to be a disruptive element in your life now? Do you feel like you carry anger around that doesn't feel heard or validated? Do you have anger about certain themes in your life that feel perpetually unresolved? These may be signs of an angry child mode demanding care.

- The *impulsive child* is triggered by a need for emotional comforting and validation, only to be met with indulgent satisfactions ("I deserve this since I never get what I want anyway!").

- The *undisciplined or rebellious child* is triggered by themes of coercion ("You can't make me do it!") or feeling betrayed and neglected ("You don't care anyway, so why should I try?") or some combination of these.

Writing Prompts

You may have more than one coping child mode, so take them one at a time as you respond to these prompts.

- Start by thinking about when you experience vulnerability, anger, impulsiveness, being undisciplined, or rebelliousness in your adult life now. As you imagine these states in the present, can you link them to memories of experiencing these emotions as a child? Write some observations of how you experience these emotions in your life now.

- Next, think about how you experienced the negative emotions in childhood. Look over your notes in your journal about your unmet needs from chapter 2 and look again at your childhood photo. As a child, how did you experience vulnerability, anger, impulsiveness, being undisciplined or rebelliousness? In the presence of others or secretly? Passively or actively?

- Now compare your present experience of vulnerability, anger, impulsiveness, being undisciplined, or rebelliousness to childhood, and write down your observations. Is there a consistent theme to what angers you from childhood to now? Write down your thoughts. That may tell you about your coping child modes.

- With each coping child mode you are considering, try to picture what it looks like. For example: What does your angry child look like when angry? How are they dressed? What age are they? What is their body language, behavior, and style of communicating like?

Difficult Coping Mode

If you're having trouble getting a fix on a mode during this exercise, it may be because you are in this mode most of the time, or it is what I would call your "baseline mode." So it makes sense that it would be hard to notice, just like asking a fish to notice the water it lives in. The following prompts are designed to help overcome this problem as much as possible.

Writing Prompts

You may have more than one difficult coping category—compliant surrenderer, detached protector, detached self-soother, self-aggrandizer, the bully—so take each subcategory one at a time as you follow these prompts.

- Where and when do you believe this mode is triggered and influences you? Be sure to include your personal life and career contexts. If you are usually in this mode, try to note the situations when you are not in this mode.

- What feelings and behaviors do you engage in when in this mode?

- What thoughts go through your mind in this mode, and if they were a script, what would it sound like?

- How do you believe the mode may be a problem for you? How is it not helping?

- Ask the mode: In your opinion, how do you help me?

- Try picturing this mode as a person, it could be a version of you, or someone who looks different. How does this person dress; what is their facial expression; how do they talk? What's it like to be around them?

Inner Critic Mode

The inner critic reveals itself in the demanding and punitive themes in your thinking and reactions as you experience them in daily life. The inner critic has a tone that you can feel. It may be an edge of meanness and anger or tone of impatience and intolerance. When you experience yourself in this mode, you may feel that angry, mean edge, but you'll also, at the same time, feel the anxiety or dread of being on the receiving end of it. I've designed the following prompts to help you get a sense of how prevalent your inner critic is in your day and how much you rely on it. (Part of the challenge of managing the inner critic is being able to claim values like ambition, discipline, and standards without having to be mean about them.)

Writing Prompts

- Are you able to notice if and when you're being mean to yourself? If you had to mark on a notepad each time you were mean to yourself, how many marks would be on the pad at the end of a typical day?

- Does the sound of your inner critic voice remind you of anyone? If so, who? What was your relationship like with this person? How did it feel to be around them, and what did you want or need from them?

- How much do you believe in your inner critic? Do you feel like it's best for you to follow its advice?

- If you woke up tomorrow and your inner critic was gone, how would you feel?

Completing Your Mode Chart

Now that you have a better idea of your modes, you can make a simple list of them by drawing the chart below in your journal or downloading the "Mode Chart" worksheet, available at http://www.newharbinger .com/50997. You can certainly use the mode labels as they are listed here, but some people prefer their own nickname. The inner critic may be "boss in the head" or the detached protector may be "robot me." Feel free to play around with your terms so you feel more ownership of them.

Mode Type These are all the modes that come between your inner child and your healthy caring adult.	Your Version This may include the nickname of your coping child, subtypes of coping child, any of the difficult coping modes, and the nickname for your inner critic, if you have one.
Coping child	
Difficult coping	
Inner critic	

Remember, these modes are the main characters that evolved out of your origin story. You're going to be getting to know them well! They will pretty much be with you for life, and they'll be triggered in stressful situations you might find yourself in. How you learn to take care of them will decide how smoothly you all get along. Sometimes people react negatively to seeing their modes. They say, "When do I get rid of them?" I think that's actually a very understandable response. People want to get rid of burdensome, painful symptoms and obstacles in life. But these particular obstacles are actually part of you, and they're shaped by pretty pivotal experiences you've had. And so, as I've been saying throughout this book, you will overcome these obstacles by making friends with these modes—and, for the more difficult ones, by knowing how to handle them assertively and productively.

The bright side of your origin story and these characters is that they tell you what you need, how you love, and what you feel. These are the ingredients to living a fulfilling life.

Prior to reading this book, your interaction with your different parts was mostly subconscious, but now with an understanding of your schemas and modes (voila!), you are more aware of the self-dialogue that's always been part of you. Getting familiar with your modes as a group is the next step.

Exercise: How to Visualize Your Modes and the Ways They Interact

For this exercise, you might start by downloading the "Theater of Your Personality Mode Map" that's available at http://www.newharbinger.com/50997. The map will really help you here. As you'll see in a moment, the instructions that follow will guide your imagination—and the map will help you visualize what you're working through in this exercise.

Imagine a theater stage (Roediger et al. 2018, 41). This can be any stage you like, say, the stage from your elementary school, from a fancy Broadway theater, or from your imagination, as long as you can picture it vividly. Now, I'm going to introduce characters for you to imagine who appear one-by-one on stage, until the complete group is assembled.

First imagine that you are sitting in the front row as a spectator. The lights come on, and you see a child center stage. The child is upset, sad, bothered, and perhaps even crying. This is your inner child, so imagine Little

You there as you have in previous exercises. You can fill in the star on the map with your name for Little You (if you have given them a name).

Next on stage walks your coping child mode. This may just be one kid, such as your vulnerable child, or it may be more than one: your angry child, your impulsive child, your undisciplined or rebellious child, or whatever name you gave them. Your coping child (or children) is standing between you and your inner child, who is behind them. Remember to see your coping child mode with all the qualities you imagined in the profiles you did earlier. You can fill in the circles on the map with any subcategories of the coping child mode.

A group of adults come on stage now and stand in front of the coping child (or children). These adults represent your difficult coping categories, however many you have. You can imagine them looking and behaving the way they did in when you read the profiles (compliant surrenderer, detached protector, detached self-soother, self-aggrandizer, bully). They may even be talking to you. One of the adults may be saying, "I just try to do whatever I need to please everyone else and try to ignore those kids." Another adult might be saying, "There's really no need to worry about them, just pretend they aren't there, and it will be better for everyone involved." Another one is ignoring the kids *and* you, possibly on their phone and social media, totally checked out. Another adult may be telling you how good they are, clearly trying to impress and intimidate you. And the last one is straight-up giving you a hard time: "What are you doing sitting there staring at us anyway? This is none of your business!" Fill in your difficult coping modes on the mode map.

Finally, to form the final row closest to you as you sit in theater, your inner critic walks out on stage. DUN-dun-dun! It may be saying: "That kid is trouble, a real pain. Little You is lazy, weak, and not worth the attention." Or: "Little You just isn't good enough; they have to be smarter; they have to be better than everyone else if they want to survive. If I don't nag them nothing will get done, and then where will you be?" They may just be yelling at your inner child at the back of the stage or arguing with your rebellious child mode, making things worse. If you have a particular term of endearment for your inner critic, write it in the triangle on the map.

Picture all the characters on the stage: a sad little kid, protected by an angry kid and a rebellious kid, surrounded by strange-acting adults who aren't helping and, in fact, are making things worse. As a play, there's a lot of drama happening here. The kid way in the back needs you; next to them, another kid is yelling or screaming and stamping their feet. The adults are in various states of drama going back and forth with the kids or even attacking you, the spectator. This is all happening, every day, on the stage of experience we all call our *personality*, with the different personality parts—our modes—making up the characters and plot of this play.

So where is the hero who comes to the rescue? This kid, Little You, is in trouble, and who's coming to save them?

You guessed it. You are.

You're going to get on the stage and learn to deal with each of these troublesome adults, getting past them one-by-one, then the coping child modes, until you can reach Little You, your inner child, and give them the care, soothing, validation, listening, support, and affection they've needed all along. This'll be you in your *healthy caring adult mode*.

There are variations of this imagery exercise. You might prefer imagining that your healthy caring adult is driving a minivan and managing all the modes in the backseats. You might even get used to having the modes around and picture them all together with you wherever you are when they're triggered. I suggest you start with the theater map until you get the hang of working with them.

In day-to-day life, you'll start to notice the modes interact with each other in different combinations. For example, the inner critic and angry coping child very often fight with each other, leaving you helplessly watching from the sidelines. Maybe your detached protector is there too, telling you to ignore it all. As you develop your healthy caring adult, you will feel more confidence to intervene.

Right now, this all may sound far-fetched, but once it becomes second nature, you'll be in a flow with your modes—and taking care of them, rather than being controlled by them. It just takes practice.

Exercise: Visualizing with Your Modes

Part 1

Referring to the "Theater of Your Personality Mode Map," try to bring the chart to life as a scene in your mind. Close your eyes and picture your inner child on the stage and slowly surround your inner child with your other modes, including any coping child modes, the difficult coping modes, and your inner critic. Freeze this image and keep it in your mind for reference.

With your personalized scene in mind, take some notes in response to these questions:

- How does it feel to look at this scene? Is this a play you would want to watch?

- Do you identify with any of the people on stage in particular?

- What thoughts and feelings do you have toward your inner child, seeing Little You surrounded by this group of characters?

These thoughts and feelings will give you an idea of how you feel about yourself overall, as well as about this project of developing insight and self-awareness. You are visualizing your personality and its parts, and how you were impacted by your history and family experience. It's a lot!

At this point, you can move to part 2 of the exercise.

Part 2

Now that you have a clear scene with your modes in mind, imagine experiencing a triggering event, how this would look with all your modes, and more importantly, how it would sound as the modes talk. This is like running through a dramatic scene with all your characters to see how the group reacts to schema triggering. To help, you may want a copy of your "Theater of Personality Mode Map" worksheet handy, and I suggest using a copy of your childhood photo too. Also, have a copy of your "Schema Chart" worksheet from chapter 3 for reference.

You'll start with a triggering event. I provide an example below, which you can use. But if you think of an example of a triggering event from your life, that will be even better. (You'll be doing more of that in the coming chapters.)

This triggering event will help you imagine which of your schemas may be triggered and which modes respond. I want you to try this because this is like dipping a toe in the process of self-awareness that's going to lead to more in-depth change.

Triggering Event Example

Imagine your boss, supervisor, or an important client calls you and sounds concerned about a project that means a lot to you: "I'm really not sure this is working out the way you've put it together. I'm not sure you quite understand my vision for this project. But I want to try to make it work. Can we meet later?"

After you say yes, she hangs up without saying good-bye.

Name Your Modes

Start with the feelings evoked in you by this event. What do you feel in your gut? What's your reaction?

For example, you may be feeling:

- anger that you aren't being appreciated

- sadness that you aren't good at your job

- guilt that you're bad at your job

- confused, hurt, or betrayed that your boss or client is doing this

- irritated that your boss is so incompetent, yet makes so many demands, and a sense you can do better than this job.

Now look at your "Schema Chart" (from chapter 3) and try to see which schemas are triggered for you. From here, you can look at your "Theater of Your Personality Mode Map" and decide which of your modes would likely react to this event.

How are you reacting? What unhelpful coping skills are you defaulting to? Are you:

- detaching from the event, telling yourself it will be fine, and just continuing as before?

- attacking yourself with criticism?

- angrily emailing your boss to tell her how unfair she's being?

- panicking and worrying you'll be fired?

- pulling an all-nighter?

- thinking there has been a miscommunication, that you and your boss have a good relationship, and that you can iron this out because you know you do good work?

Note which modes are triggered for you. Remember to start with how your inner child would feel and whether there are coping child categories, difficult coping categories, or inner critic aspects triggered. Just make a list.

What Do Your Modes Sound Like?

Now we're going to take the modes triggered from this exercise and try to imagine what they would say in reaction to the triggering event. I'll give examples, starting with what might be the loudest voices first.

Detached protector: "You don't need to worry about this. You really don't need this client anyway, so who cares? She probably doesn't know what she's talking about, or she's overreacting, so you don't need to take her seriously. Just humor her and go along with what she's saying, but it doesn't matter. You can just pretend this isn't touching you. You may be feeling upset about it inside, but nobody needs to see that, it will just make you look bad."

Inner critic: "Oh, great, more proof that you can't do your freaking job. It's like I'm always telling you: it's amazing you're still employed here. You should really pay attention to the criticism or you're just going to keep screwing up. But whatever, at the end of the day, everyone will see that you're a failure."

Vulnerable child: "Oh no. I feel so worthless. This client is going to reject me and tell me I'm not good enough. Maybe she doesn't even need me. She might even tell my coworkers, and I'll be rejected by everyone. I'm so scared. I feel so alone."

Angry child: "I hate this! Every time I try to do something, you tell me I'm no good! Maybe I shouldn't even try anymore. I hate you (inner critic) for always riding me, and I hate my client for bringing this up in the first place!"

Now, try to write the script for each of your triggered modes and what they would say to this trigger (or your own trigger you are working with), along the lines of the examples. Use a sheet from your journal and write lines for each of your modes.

How Do Modes Talk to Each Other?

Next, let's go one step further and imagine how these modes would talk to each other if they were in a room together or on a stage. It's a bit like writing a screenplay. And our modes actually do interact this way. Here's an example:

Detached protector (to all modes): "None of you matter. You are a distraction; I wish you weren't talking at all. Your feelings don't matter. The point here is that nothing has to touch us, and we will manage better that way. This client doesn't matter, and neither do you all. We can do without all of you. If you listen to me and shut up, you'll be safe."

Angry child (to detached protector): "You're such a jerk. I'm going to fight you on this because I should be telling that client to shut up! This job sucks, and I'm sick of being pushed around! I can't just be me and do a good job."

Inner critic (to angry child): "This is typical. You're out of control and ruining everything. We would all be better off if you would just go away. You're unacceptable. You ruin everything."

Vulnerable child (to themself): "I feel so bad; it feels like I ruin every-thing. I don't deserve to have anyone's help. I'm such a failure. But it's so painful to be here alone and feeling rejected. I'm scared."

Now just like before, use your list of modes to write a script for how they would likely talk to each other after the triggering event, just like the examples above.

How to Consistently Cope in an Adaptive Way

I know this may seem like a lot of talking from one stressful interaction at work, but if you focus on the different and often contradicting emotions you feel in response as well as the mindsets that happen and then amplify them into voices, you'll get something like this—this particular mix of voices, speaking to and across each other, jostling to express their feelings and fears and to get their needs met.

So why is it important to label modes and listen for their differing voices? When you look at this scene and the triggering that might be involved in a situation like this, what do you think it might ultimately translate to if the triggered modes were not recognized and dealt with? I would predict that the detached protector is going to remain in charge, and during the discussion with the client, you'd somehow make a bad impression. Maybe you, in defensive, detached protector mode, wouldn't really listen to the client's feedback or authentically advocate for your-self; you'd turn off and proceed robotically through the conversation instead. This may leave the client unimpressed, the two of you still at loggerheads, and possibly ruin things. That, in turn, would only give the inner critic more ammunition to attack you and make the inner child feel worse and the angry child bitter.

Ultimately, if you were in a situation like this, it'd be better to have a more authentic interaction with the client, without feeling threat-ened, and confidently negotiate a solution to the problem that still left your boundaries and professionalism as an employee respected. You might also need to recognize and accept any feelings of insecurity or stress as a result of this situation—after all, it's never pleasant to be criticized or forced back to the drawing board, even when we respond to it as confidently as we can—so these feelings aren't displaced in the rest of your life in other ways: say, by you getting mad at your spouse or partner later in the evening, after work, or through patterns like binge-ing, checking-out in front of the TV, or other distractions, and more.

But as it stands in your life now, your modes likely aren't letting that happen. They aren't stepping back in the way you need them to in order to be able to cope well *consistently*, even when life is hard. And so, what you need is another mode that can come in and calm all the others down and find a way to feel confident to talk with the client—or deal adaptively with whatever it is you face in life that stresses you out and makes coping hard. And that new mode is the healthy caring adult, which you will learn more about next!

Chapter 5

Bringing It All Together with the Healthy Caring Adult Mode

You've learned a lot about yourself, right? You have charts for your temperament, your schemas, and your modes, and you have a clear sense of your inner child based on your childhood photos. The big question now is, How does all of this help you?

If you want to tackle a problem and make change, it's crucial to look at the problem from a place of clarity, where you can see what's happening. You need to have some distance from the problem, so you are in a better position to understand and take effective action.

By building a *healthy caring adult mode,* you are developing the clarity and the ability to observe yourself from a distance while you are triggered in one of your modes.

This may sound kind of impossible, like saying, "You have to be you and not be you at the same time." To be more accurate though, it's like saying that you can become two versions of yourself in order to change: the triggered you and your ideal you. And like everything in schema therapy, we want those two versions of you to talk to each other!

People Study: A Picture of the Healthy Caring Adult

Let's reconnect with Judy, whom you met in chapter 1. Due to an emotionally absent father and a mother who used a punitive, impatient tone with Judy throughout her childhood, she is coping with defectiveness and failure schemas. Judy's main coping modes include the demanding inner critic, responsible for her rigid character at work (effective and successful, but mostly free of pleasure); the detached protector, who fights to keep her away from emotions; and the detached self-soother who has her zone out in her private time and rely on alcohol. We can deepen our understanding of Judy as we connect with her coping child modes. Her vulnerable child feels the pain of isolation and loneliness, which is enforced by the detached protector and detached self-soother, as well as the rejection at the hands of the demanding inner critic, making the vulnerable child feel rejected and flawed. When Judy is alone, often in the morning while showering or on the weekends when drinking, the angry, rebellious child comes out, sick of all the demands and discipline and wanting to at least indulge in physical pleasures, like food and drinking, and avoid work.

As Judy got into her early thirties, she began to hit bottom with the stuckness that her detachment had led her into. She considered whether she would ever build a social life and start dating and meet someone for a serious relationship. She sometimes even wondered about having a family. She was certainly growing impatient with spending weekends alone, her inner child longed for more love and connection, and Judy had only her work routine to look forward to. She needed a way out.

After learning her schemas and modes—let's say after using this book—Judy was able to consciously connect with her needs, values, and strengths. She painfully realized that she had let years pass without giving herself and her inner child what she needed in life and that now she deserved more. She understood she has an inner child who wants more fun, play, warmth, and affection and needs to be released from the pain of rejection she feels. She reminded herself of her strengths: that she values strong relationships and loyalty, and that kindness is important to her. She knew her life would feel empty, regardless of how successful she was in her career, if she didn't have deep friendships and maybe a love relationship. Judy recognized that when she wasn't struggling with the urge to detach, she actually liked people and enjoyed being around them! She can be silly and has a keen sense of humor when her guard is down. So she took ownership of her ambition, hardworking nature, and drive without assuming they had to be part of a punishing, demanding, grim outlook. She came to understand that if she put her mind to being in the healthy caring adult mode and fighting to take care of her inner child, she had the guts to try to succeed.

Judy began to connect with the healthy caring adult mode once she made the decision to take on the responsibility of improving her life, considering that she might even deserve that. Clearer on her values and strengths, she put together an image of herself as a compassionate, patient, nurturing, but also disciplined adult. She even made this image real by holding onto a photo of her adult self, looking happy and lively. Now she had a vision of her healthy caring adult mode. She would rely on this image of herself to give her the courage to face emotional and experiential challenges she had spent her life avoiding. She turned her journal into a healthy caring adult journal with that photo on the inside cover. She took notes on her goals and documented the challenges she faced along with her successes and wins.

Judy also learned how to develop a voice to talk back to her modes and connect with her inner child. After some practice, she came to appreciate and even enjoy the dialogue, finding humor in it at times, as well as the fulfillment of deep emotional awareness.

The Healthy Caring Adult Mode in Action

Let's take a glimpse into what it looks like to work with the healthy caring adult mode. Judy scheduled a first date with someone she had been chatting with on a dating app. On the night of her date, she got home from work, and her modes were giving her a hard time. "You don't have to do this; it's probably not going to work out anyway. Why put yourself through it? Better to just ghost the guy and binge-watch *Call My Agent*." Judy stood at the door holding her keys, gazing past a potted fern in the hallway, and said to herself, "You can't detach your way out of this. It's scary, I know that. But this is not about the rejection I grew up with. I'm an adult now, and I know I'm a good, loveable person. I will handle myself well and the stakes don't have to be so high. Believe it or not, I'm going to go have a good time tonight. And if it doesn't work out, I may have a good story to tell." In her self-talk, Judy brushed past the detached protector and connected with her vulnerable child, who was afraid of more rejection.

Then, Judy's inner critic piped up, making her feel tense and anxious. "I don't think you'll be what this guy is looking for. You never are." Again, her healthy caring adult stepped in and told the critic to back off: "I know you have high standards and want us to succeed, but you really aren't helping with this tone. I deserve better than that. Time to back off!"

In the car on the way to the restaurant, Judy used brief mindful imagery to picture her healthy caring adult with her vulnerable child—whose rejection anxiety, she knew, was what was kicking the detached protector and the inner critic into action. In the image, they always meet in a Dairy Queen from her childhood, over soft-serve vanilla ice cream with rainbow sprinkles. "I know that critic makes you feel bad, like you aren't good enough, and it hurts, like you're alone. I want you to remember you don't have to listen to her. You know that, right? I know better than her, and I can tell you that you are a great kid, worth loving, and funny and talented. I won't let you forget it, I'm always in your corner. You deserve good things." This soothing and reassuring helped Judy transform the vulnerable child into a healthy inner child with clear needs for love, without fear.

A key element of mode dialogue is the special relationship between the healthy caring adult and the inner child. This is the core of therapeutic action and where change in the schema therapy approach occurs since the source of most schema triggering starts with the inner child before the modes kick in. Remember the diagram of modes on a stage in the theater. The point of that diagram is to illustrate what comes between the healthy caring adult and the inner child: all the modes in between. Once dialogue happens between the adult and that inner child, you know you've successfully embarked on the recovery process.

Once your healthy caring adult enters the scene, your inner child has a chance, sometimes for the first time in your life, to share core feelings in a safe environment. And you provide this safety for yourself, which is a powerful deepening of self-esteem. Once you start to feel the benefits of this approach, you will intuitively use it—and use it more often—because it feels good! And this becomes a virtuous cycle: the more you practice, the better you get; the better you feel, the more you use it.

How to Understand the Healthy Caring Adult Mode

Let's start with the term "healthy adult." Do those words make you picture someone super organized, successful, and effective? Possibly the word "adult" gives a sense that they are uptight and kind of intimidating? I add the word "caring" to the term, so we don't forget the element of an ideal parent for the self, someone with compassion.

You can see from Judy's story that the healthy caring adult plays a few roles at once. The healthy caring adult:

- is an *ideal parent* who cares for your inner child and sets limits with the coping child, difficult coping, and inner critic modes

- holds the *values* that are part of who you want to be

- has a *healthy perspective* you can take outside of your modes and moods

- shows *confidence* by bringing bravery and resolve, kindness, and generosity to the situations you find yourself in.

The key to the healthy caring adult mode is doing it in your own way, with your own style and variations. That is, what your healthy caring adult mode looks like will depend on the kind of person you are. If you're naturally more edgy in your tone and you like it like that, you should embrace that with compassion. In fact, this process—of changing the ways you interpret events and the ways you cope or deal with them—only works if you feel ownership of it and if you actually like your healthy caring adult mode and enjoy spending time with it. As you start to focus on your healthy caring adult, you will see that you already have a lot of healthy caring adult traits; thinking in terms of your healthy caring adult mode basically means visualizing those traits in one place. You will also visualize and cultivate new qualities that you value.

So the healthy caring adult is two things at the same time: a state of mind you can get into as well as the journey you take to get into that state of mind. In other words, it's like already being in the place you're traveling to.

It can also help to realize that ultimately, inhabiting the healthy caring adult mode boils down to one thing: voice. The healthy caring adult in action is a voice and a position you speak from, and that's really it. You speak to yourself and your modes in the single voice, bringing together the ideal parent, a placeholder of values, a healthy perspective, and confidence.

It's quite common for my clients to ask me, "How do you get this healthy caring adult voice?" and I always explain that it starts with the decision to do it. This is harder than it sounds because our brains are so set in their ways. But once you take the first step toward understanding and inhabiting the voice of your healthy caring adult mode, all you have to do is practice. In my experience, it's exactly like learning a musical instrument. However accomplished a musician may be, they practice the same way through all levels of development. And, as a musician moves from beginner to professional, they practice pretty much the same amount every day, every week; they commit to practice, and they're consistent with it.

It Starts with the Inner Child

Since you've made it this far into this book, I know you are committed to making change in your life. At the same time, your coping modes may still be the ones driving you to improve, wanting you to be more effective or perfect, and so on. There is a part of you who wants you to feel better but doesn't know how to get there: the inner child. The inner child is the source of your authentic feelings and needs, the part of you trying to feel better. The challenge is that your inner child can only ask you to change and hope you will. Like any child, your inner child doesn't have authority. That child needs to rely on an adult who has the power to help. You take on the responsibility of playing the healthy caring adult role. And when we spend most of our life in coping modes, we spend more time ignoring our inner child than we do listening. Think back to the "Theater of the Personality Mode Map" and recall the modes as obstacles between the healthy caring adult and the inner child.

The healthy caring adult's first appearance on the stage begins with you saying you will get into that role and take on that authority. Some people find occupying the authority in this role more complicated than others, and that's totally okay. Think of it like getting a promotion to a leadership role at work or realizing you are in fact the main character in the story—a story in which a child is depending on you. There are characters (modes) who want to get in your way, and you are taking on the responsibility of managing those modes. This means developing the confidence to have loving authority toward yourself.

How Healthy and Caring Is Your Adult Self?

You may be feeling in touch with your desire to feel better and do better and see that as a good start to connecting with your healthy caring adult. It can take some time to get out of the habit of assuming that your conscious mind, right now, is your ally, and that when you are at your most rational, you are taking care of yourself. Because these points are definitely not always true. It can take some time to develop a fully compassionate and accepting approach to yourself, so bear the following questions in mind.

I want you to journal your answers now, but also leave room to answer them again. At the end of this chapter, I'll ask you to answer them a second time.

- Think about yourself with the flaws and imperfections you have right now. Do you deserve all the happiness and fulfillment you are looking for? Or do you respond to this question with the idea that you have "a lot of work to do first"? What other reactions come up for you?

- Imagine that you can take action right now to do something about your feelings, whatever that may be. Maybe you know that it's possible to feel better than you currently do, but the price is a lot of discomfort—changing behavior is hard and brings up tough feelings. How willing are you to do that? If you're not that willing, deep down, what's stopping you? What feelings come up?

- How important is it for you to make changes in your life? If you imagine yourself living your best life, what are you doing? How valuable is that to you?

- Check in with yourself now. How confident do you feel and how much of a sense of caring authority over yourself, your emotions, and your actions do you feel when answering these questions?

Getting Comfortable Being the Healthy Caring Adult with Your Inner Child

As you continue to notice your schemas being triggered and your coping modes reacting, you're going to get better and better at seeing the hurt and vulnerability underneath your triggering, which means you'll be seeing your inner child more often. Your relationship with your inner child mode—the dialogue you might have between the image of your child-self in your mind and the image of your healthy caring adult mode, whom you'll get to know shortly—becomes a key experience for you to care for yourself and provide for your needs. What does this look like in practice?

As you can guess, the experience involves having an image in mind and using your voice to express yourself in the image. When you feel a need and emotion, picture your child-self with the emotion, and then picture your healthy caring adult on the scene, offering care and validation.

Exercise: Healthy Caring Adult Journal

Changing ineffective coping skills involves overcoming some mindsets that have been dominant for you for most or all of your life. This means that even as you forge a new mindset, the old ones may quickly return and take over when you aren't looking. That's okay! These mindsets are really just trying to take care of you in their own way, and with patience and persistence, they will eventually get the message that you don't need them anymore. You just need to remind your brain that you're an adult and you can take it from here. A key tool to begin this work is your journal you selected for this work (as mentioned in the introduction). Your "healthy caring adult journal" (Kuyken 2009) will be a catch-all to collect pieces of your healthy caring adult experiences, which can include:

- your thoughts, feelings, and observations about your schemas and modes

- mode dialogues

- lists

- vison board images

- inspiring photos from your life

- mementos from good experiences and accomplishments

- fragments of creative expression.

As you proceed with piecing together your healthy caring adult, your coping modes are going to try to erase important bits of work or experiences and fold them back into the status quo. The journal will help you prevent that from happening, so each time you look at it, you are reminded of your healthy caring adult mode and the good things you are capable of. Your journal is going to become documented proof of you becoming a new you. Through the exercise in chapter, you'll continue filling the journal with good things.

You'll start with picture of healthy Adult You. I'd like you to find a photo of yourself that you feel good about. Preferably a photo from a time in your adult life when you felt proud of yourself. Print it out and attach it right on the first page.

Keep your journal handy so you can record meaningful observations or experiences. As people become clearer about their healthy caring adult as a placeholder of their ideal self, a key question that comes up in life situations both small and large is: "What are my values? What's important to me?" Values become an important compass for you while you grow as a more self-aware person.

Healthy Caring Adult Values

As your healthy caring adult begins to influence the direction of your life in deep ways, you will find that you will need to be more aware of what you value about being you (Roediger et al. 2018, 41). That is, once you begin to overcome the influence of your modes and question them, you'll need to decide how you would rather live and what's really important to you. This always comes up as people make progress with their modes, and it's a good idea to prepare with a discussion on values.

My schema therapy approach to values begins with the assumption that your coping modes influence your sense of values in ways that may *not* be helpful to you and, in fact, that muddy the water and cause strife. When thinking about values, you're vulnerable to your modes making you feel badly about yourself or skewing your sense of the reasonable and real. That's why identifying your values needs to account for your modes first.

But wait! Before you go further, I want to remind you that this exercise isn't about forcing you to adopt values that aren't part of your character. Your modes are still part of you and your history and inform your identity. What you *are* doing is tempering your modes by bringing them *more* in line with your position as an independent adult. In other words, you are updating your values. I think you'll find you feel more ownership of your values after going through this process.

For example, instead of resorting to the values of a demanding inner critic, you can try to temper your demands with measured ambition. "I find a lot of fulfillment in being the best at what I do. I know that I don't always have to be the best and that part of succeeding is having some small failures along the way, which I learn from. So I never know when a failure may be part of a larger success."

As you read the above, you may have been thinking, *Easy for him to say!* I know. It's one thing to do this abstractly, but when you come to your own modes and bringing a different perspective to your values, it's not so easy. So I want to get you started with some examples that may be helpful, which have been widely adopted by my clients.

The Six Principles of the Healthy Caring Adult

The healthy caring adult cares for the inner child first and deals with all the challenges that child faces. In this light, the principles of good parenting inspire a helpful reflection on values.

Think about the responsibilities a parent has and how to manage those responsibilities. (Even if you don't have children of your own, you can play along.) It takes attention, practice, effort, patience, resilience, boundaries, and the ability to have fun too. Ultimately, responsible parenting means using a particular mindset and set of skills with a precious relationship in your life, that is, the one with your children. Responsible parents nurture that relationship as they nurture the children. Now imagine having this same attitude and approach toward yourself. You're taking a position of responsibility for a previous relationship in your life: you.

In order to hone and visualize your healthy caring adult values, I'd like to bring you back to your "Theater of the Personality Mode Map." When you look at the map, you see your inner child at the top of the page (or back of the stage) and all the reactive coping child, difficult coping, and inner critic modes separating you from your child-self. The goal is to bring your healthy caring adult on stage with the inner child, kneeling down to be close, being a good parent, and taking care. This means dealing with all the other modes in ways that your child-self has never been able to, just as a parent protects a child from overwhelming challenges in the world so the child can focus on learning and facing age-appropriate growth tasks.

There's a catch. Your difficult coping mode, sometimes your coping child mode, and their thoughts must certainly blend with your conscious, self-aware healthy caring adult thoughts—they are, after all, inhabiting the same person—so it may be confusing as you are finding your way as a healthy caring adult. For example, what's the difference between valuing ambition and being overdemanding?

Also, you may have difficult coping or inner critic modes that dominate your thinking to such an extent that it may take more effort to connect with your inner child and coping child mode. In these cases, you may ask yourself, "Who am I when I'm not detached or demanding?" At times like this, your healthy caring adult plays the role of nurturing your inner child on the path of unhindered exploration, expression, and validation of feelings. This is also where those healthy parenting values we talked about come into play to help guide you when mode thinking blurs your outlook.

I've put together six basic principles of being a healthy caring adult. Experiment with using these principles like a compass to guide you through differentiating your healthy caring adult from your coping child, difficult coping, and inner critic modes (Steinberg 2004).

The healthy caring adult is:

1. *curious and accepting:* notices, encourages, and accepts feelings and needs

2. *a self-advocate:* communicates feelings and asserts needs

3. *confident:* shows authority

4. *protective and firm:* sets limits when necessary

5. *generous:* considers others' feelings and needs without worrying about their own

6. *kind and caring:* notices punitiveness and rigidity and replaces them with caring ambition, support, and affection.

As you can see, these principles are based on managing difficult coping modes and introducing elements of being firm, forthright, compassionate, actively caring, and sensitive as situations and your modes demand. You'll find your own way of expressing these principles in your mind, in your own words, which will guide how you treat yourself by dealing with modes (which is why documenting your new principles in the journal will help).

Returning to your "Theater of the Personality Mode Map," you'll see that if you approach any of your modes using the above six principles, you will have an attitude that can break through the mode thinking that can get so convincing, whether it means setting limits for the angry child, noticing the punitive tone of the inner critic, or catching the absence of emotion when you are in a detached zone. In the next chapter, I'll introduce you to some exercises that will help you practice working with your new healthy adult attitude.

Now let's deepen your sense of your healthy caring adult with some more work on your journal.

Exercise: Your Healthy Caring Adult Values

Now that you have an idea of the role values play in your personal strengths and resilience, as well as a cautionary note on the influences of difficult coping modes, you can think through what you find important in life. This is another page to add to your journal.

For this exercise you'll be a making a list of the values you just contemplated. This exercise should help you get more clarity on the conflicts you experience around who you want to be and how your modes are getting in the way.

You'll be using two sections for your values: internally focused values and externally focused values.

Start with a page in your journal and see how detailed and lengthy your list gets; use as much space as you like. Use the list below as writing prompts. So just copy each item into your journal and see where you go as you write about it. There are nine items, so you should have nine responses written in your journal when you're done.

Values with an external focus:

- love relationships

- family or chosen family

- friendships

- career

- identity and social values (ideals for how you treat others and live in community).

Values with an internal focus:

- hobbies

- physical and mental health

- spirituality and love

- personal values (ideals for how you treat yourself).

Okay, as you were working on this list, you may have noticed some conflict happening in your mind or emotions, perhaps thoughts like, *Is this good enough?* or *This should be more ambitious*, or *I know I should want to do this, but I don't!* You may have noticed a feeling of stress or pressure as you wrote. These are signs of conflict between your modes and your newly forming healthy caring adult. This is okay—in fact, you actually want this to happen, so you learn more about where your difficult coping mode conflicts are. In the next chapter, you're going to practice how your healthy caring adult will manage your difficult coping modes and keep you fulfilled.

The Healthy Caring Adult Is a Process in Your Life

Let's talk about some adjustments in perspective that come with this approach to life. Remember that your healthy caring adult is not a perfect ideal, but a real person with feelings: you in the adult world. That means you in a complicated world with challenges, problems, and pain, as well as joy and accomplishment. The healthy caring adult is a process of being open, real, creative, and compassionate as well as flawed and human. The key to getting it is the word "process." As long as your trying, you're there.

The experience of healthy caring adult as a process plays out in limitless ways, and here are some important points to keep in mind:

- A common reaction to the healthy caring adult concept is "If I learn to be so self-sufficient and caring with myself, does that mean I don't need other people?" If you're playing the role of healthy caring adult for an internal lonely or neglected child, you're soothing that child and validating the pain, but you're also advocating for that child and courageously going out in the world to connect with others and provide for yourself the love that you need.

- Another common question about the healthy caring adult goes something like this: "If I'm angry or sad, is it always a mode—do feelings always mean that I'm triggered in a traumatized way?" While a lot of our primary emotions, such as fear, sadness, and joy, come from core childhood sources, these feelings don't automatically mean a mode is triggered. We live in a world with misfortune, frustration, and even malice. For example, if you are coping with structural violence on a larger scale, a racist microaggression in your day, or your male workplace peers being paid more than you, you have real adult reasons to feel anger and want fairness. If a loved one suddenly falls ill or is in an accident, you may feel worry, fear, grief, or anger, but these may not be triggered by difficult coping modes. The process of being the healthy caring adult means you are in a mindset of welcoming and validating of such emotions and coping as an adult.

• There are times, though, when a situation in your adult world triggers a difficult coping mode to overreact to what's happening—it's a child's reaction to an adult situation. This doesn't mean your mode reaction—whether a coping child or difficult coping mode—is *wrong*, but that it's just misplaced in time. And it's up to your healthy caring adult to catch that and care for the triggered inner child while handling the situation as an adult. Leave the work to adult you!

• An unexpected but crucial element to the change process is the fact that substantial change over time *feels* different in your body, and that can take some getting used to. If you have been accustomed to certain kinds of triggered emotions for most of your life, it can feel odd to go through your week less triggered. You may feel a bit uneasy, like you have too much energy, which is kind of true since you're using less energy being upset! This is where your healthy caring adult, using mindfulness mediation as we'll discuss in chapter 7, will help you translate your energy into new pursuits.

Pop Quiz!

Do you recall the questions I asked you earlier in the chapter, questions about what you think you deserve from life and how your answers made you feel? Try answering them again in your journal, this time with more of a feel for healthy caring adult principles and with some added clarity on your own personal values. How much acceptance and compassion do you feel for yourself as you answer this time?

Here they are again:

- Do you deserve all the happiness and fulfillment you are looking for?

- Are you willing to take action to help yourself and your inner child? If not, what's stopping you?

- How important is it to you to make positive changes in your life?

- If you imagine yourself living your best life, what do you see? How do you feel about what you see?

- How confident and how much of a sense of caring authority do you feel when answering the above?

Try comparing your second round of answers with your first round. What kind of changes do you notice in your perspective of yourself now?

Keep these questions in mind as you continue with the rest of this book and keep your journal handy—you never know when you want to share something with yourself.

Chapter 6

Mode Dialogues Show You a New Way

Now that you have a good sense of your healthy caring adult and you're using your journal to record and process all the changes you'll be making in your life, in this chapter, you'll focus on the core reason for developing your healthy caring adult mode: so you can manage your other modes to make positive change happen.

Ultimately, the point of managing modes is to convince them to let go of being an obstacle between your healthy caring adult and your inner child. Starting in childhood, our vulnerability is shielded by our coping child and difficult coping modes, which, at the time, provided needed protection. But once we become adults, what was a wall of protection kind of becomes the wall of a prison, blocking our inner child from care and affection.

In this chapter, you'll learn to connect with and overcome your coping child and difficult coping modes so your needs feel less problematic and become an opening to get the care and attention your inner child longs for. You're going to learn a step-by-step method for doing just that.

Your healthy caring adult can dialogue with your coping child and difficult coping modes and manage them with cognitive, emotional, and behavioral tools. These tools are really just a set of self-dialogue practices to connect with your inner child, which you can use in your daily life to make real change in your moods and your behavior.

In some ways, this is this book's most important chapter for learning schema therapy self-talk skills. I can't stress enough how important the *practice* aspect is to this journey—as I say, it's like learning an instrument. I want you to be able to take these skills with you for the rest of your life—and really take the time to learn them. An invaluable part of your success will be scheduling regular practice of these skills in your day-to-day life.

Six Principles of Managing Modes with Dialogue

Once you start working with your modes, you're going to notice that they each have their own character and tone and operate like fully formed human beings (Kellogg 2015, 94–112). This may sound far-fetched, but it really works this way. Your modes pay attention in the background throughout your day, remember things, hold a grudge, and fight back. As you'll see, an important element of this process is building a bond and a trusting relationship between your healthy caring adult and your other modes (Roediger et al. 2018, 179–197). This trusting bond is based on your healthy caring adult providing validation, care, and support as well as limit-setting for all your modes. This allows your healthy caring adult to open up better communication with your inner child, which is how healing happens. You are putting into practice your ideas of being a good parent as discussed in the last chapter. Now, I will talk you through the specifics of how that sounds based on the schema therapy principles of *limited reparenting* and *empathic confrontation*.

I've taken my experience from training, supervision, and certification as a schema therapist combined with my clinical work doing mode dialogue with my clients to distill the therapeutic pattern of the dialogue process into six principles, which can be used with each type of mode. These principles are a kind of "how-to" list for how the healthy caring adult can practice engaging with the coping child and difficult coping modes, managing them, connecting with the inner child, and providing care for deep need and emotions.

Remember, your healthy caring adult is dealing with modes in order to reach your inner child and provide care. That is the ultimate goal of dialogue, which we can reach with the fifth principle below (Young et al. 2003, 298–302).

The six principles include:

1. *Connect* with the mode and get its attention.

2. Explain the mode's *goal* and validate in the context of unmet needs.

3. *Explain the harm* this mode is causing.

4. Set a *limit* for the mode behavior.

5. *Care* for the inner child with compassion, validation, and soothing.

6. *Promise* you will address the original mode goal and care for the inner child.

Practicing these principles is a great technique for cultivating your healthy caring adult (Young et al. 2003, 92–94, 182–186). As we go through the steps, it will help to bear in mind the diagram from your mode map of you as healthy caring adult trying to reach your inner child with the coping child and difficult coping modes as well as the inner critic blocking your way.

1. **Connect.** As your healthy caring adult deals with a coping child, difficult coping, or inner critic mode before being able to reach your inner child, your first challenge is to get the troublesome modes' attention (connect). This can be harder than it sounds. Think about getting the attention of, say, someone who is detached; of a child who is having a tantrum; or of a punitive, mean person who is completely sure of their opinion and not interested in what you have to say. This really is a matter of using people skills! Think of difficult people or children you have interacted with in your life and how you have to find a way to speak to them that they can hear.

2. **Goal.** Once you have your mode's attention, you're going to build your credibility with it by explaining and validating that you understand why the mode is doing what it does. You know that, during childhood, you had emotional needs, and the situation being what it was, the actions your mode has taken were the only way of managing: it was the best you could do, and even now it has a lot of upsides too. You get it.

3. **Explain the harm.** But in the end, this mode behavior ain't helping! You also have to explain to your mode how its coping behavior actually perpetuates the problems you were trying to escape. The mode is always backfiring by keeping your inner child stuck in the same kind of unhappiness and neglect you grew up with.

4. **Limit.** You're going to explain in detail how you want the mode to "back off" and specifically what behavior needs to change. And, unless you're dealing with a particularly mean inner critic mode that might need an especially stern talking to, you'll try to do this with compassion because it's more effective.

5. **Care.** This is a key step in the scene, really the heart of it all. Now is the pivot point, where you move from dealing with coping child, difficult coping, and inner critic modes to being with the inner child directly. You're meeting at last! Imagine this as the key, moving, powerful scene in the movie that wins awards. Your inner child is finally connecting with someone who is listening and who cares! And your healthy caring adult is saying the things the child needs to hear.

6. **Promise.** This is a chance to establish a long-term bond among *all* of your modes. You've finally been successful reaching your inner child and showing that you care. Now you reassure all modes involved that you have the power and authority to do things differently and get your inner child out of this painful place. You're getting all your modes, eventually, to see that you all have the same goals: what's best for you. This is an important step forward in convincing your modes they can give you a chance on a regular basis.

Remember your "Theater of the Personality Mode Map" and the three mode types that come between your healthy caring adult and inner child:

- *Coping child* (vulnerable, angry, impulsive, undisciplined/rebellious)

- *Difficult coping* (compliant surrender, detached protector, detached self-soother, self-aggrandizer, bully)

- *Inner critic* (punitive aspect, demanding aspect).

In the sections to come, you will learn to apply the six principles to each of the above three mode types and you'll practice the specifics of these principles with your particular unique modes. With each mode type, I'll give you a prompt to pull an image into your mind of the mode, which you will use when the time comes to do your own mode dialogue. (If you don't believe you have any modes within a particular mode type, you can skip it.) You'll also read a fictional background example to add some context for the dialogue. You should already know which modes you want to focus on from your "Theater of the Personality Mode Map" and have a diagram of them. I'll offer the healthy caring adult side of the dialogue and let you imagine how the inner child mode in the example may respond.

First, we'll look at some examples, and then you can do this exercise yourself. But as you're reading along, feel free to use your journal to take notes. Finally, remember that these dialogues may sound like a lot, especially in the moment your mode is triggered, but the process becomes intuitive and happens a lot more quickly with practice.

Dialogue with the Coping Child Mode

What sets this mode type apart from the others is the pronounced childlike or teen quality to it. A dialogue with the coping child mode is about relating to a child of maybe five years old or perhaps a rebellious or undisciplined child from middle-school or early-teen years. From your mode theater map, you will know whether you have a coping child mode, how old they are, their unique qualities, and what category of coping child they may be—vulnerable, angry, impulsive, undisciplined/rebellious, or your own name for it.

Image prompt. When you feel the emotions associated with this mode, what age comes to mind with the tone of the emotion or attitude? Maybe you start with body language. You feel that crossed arms makes sense or rolling on the ground in a tantrum. Connect the body language to an age. What were you like at that age? Put an image of yourself at that age with that body language in your mind. Now complete the image by taking the role of the healthy caring adult and being with this coping child mode for this dialogue.

Background. Let's say you are with your partner and telling a story from your day about something that upset you. Your partner's phone vibrates with a text message, and he checks his phone while you're in the middle of talking. This triggers an angry child, let's say around seven years old. You are tempted to yell at your partner.

1. **Connect with the mode to get its attention.** "Hey, whoa! What's going on, what happened? What's got you so upset? Let me take your hand. Let's go over here and talk for a second. Okay, can you tell me what happened?"

2. **Explain the mode's *goal* and validate in the context of unmet needs.** "I know, you're really upset, you feel like he's not paying attention to you, that makes you so angry and you want to make him pay attention! When people don't pay attention to you it makes you feel neglected and angry. And you want it to stop now! Do I have that right? I know when you were growing up, you spent a lot of time feeling like no one paid attention to you, and it really hurt. So no more of *that*, right?!"

3. ***Explain the harm* this mode is causing.** "I get why you're angry, and you can tell me all about it. But when you get this angry, you get angry with people you love, right? And the thing is, this just makes people get further away from you because it makes them angry and scared too. So you end up feeling more alone. If you yell now, it's going to be an argument, but you really needed to connect with him, right?"

4. **Set a *limit* for the mode behavior.** "I want to tell you that you can share your anger with me, I want to hear all about it, but we

can't keep lashing out at our partner. It's only going to hurt *us* more."

5. **Care for the inner child with compassion, validation, and soothing.** "I know inside you're hurt and scared, and you get angry to protect yourself. What happened wasn't what you needed; you don't like being ignored like that. You're a wonderful, loveable kid, and I won't ignore you, I will help the people you love give you what you need. You deserve it."

6. **Promise you will address the original mode goal and care for the inner child.** "I want you to know that I'm going to speak to our partner and make sure he knows we don't like this and make sure we handle things differently. Okay? I'm going to take care of you, so you don't have to feel scared and alone. I promise. I'm going to go talk to him with my adult powers, and you will see that I'm going to take care of things. Okay?"

Dialogue with the Difficult Coping Mode Categories

The categories of this mode kind of say it all: compliant surrender, detached protector, detached self-soother, self-aggrandizer, bully. The name of each mode category gives a sense of the emotional tone the mode shows and the kind of image that'll be best for it.

Example 1: Difficult Coping: Detached Protector

Image prompt. An image I like to use with the detached protector is a bouncer at a club. We're talking to someone with their arms folded, in front of the door, not letting anyone in. But you can find an image that works better for you.

Background. Let's work with the idea that you were just disappointed by a friend. You were having an argument with your romantic partner and felt really upset. You reached out to your friend for support, so you texted her, and she didn't get back to you. Now the detached protector wants nothing to do with it. Your impulse is to ignore your friend and tell yourself it never pays to trust people. Just forget the whole thing.

1. *Connect* **with the mode to get its attention.** "You're really disconnecting right now. I can see you're turning your back on your friend. She blew it, and this is what she gets, is that it?"

2. **Explain the mode's *goal* and validate in the context of unmet needs.** "Look, I get why you are putting up these walls. It's like you're standing in the doorway and not letting anyone in. And why shouldn't you? Growing up, you got hurt over and over by people who were supposed to be there for you and to love you. Anyone in your place would feel the same way—I would feel the same way. You didn't deserve that. I know how much people hurt you, and you're trying to keep that from happening again."

3. *Explain the harm* **this mode is causing.** "But here's the thing: if we keep putting up these walls, your loved ones aren't ever going to get a chance to get close. People are imperfect, and they disappoint us, but we can still love them and be open to them. By keeping these walls up, you're also putting that kid who grew up disappointed into a prison, and you're like the jailer."

4. **Set a *limit* for the mode behavior.** "Let's try something. I want you to give me a chance to protect this kid, but in a way that doesn't make him feel alone and isolated. I don't want that for him. So we are going to text our friend and make sure she saw the text we sent last night and tell her we could really use a talk. This time, we aren't going to pretend we don't have feelings."

5. **Care for the inner child with compassion, validation, and soothing.** "Now let me take care of Little You for a while; I think it will help you feel better. We can just try it out if you like."

   Say to your inner child: "I know you've been really hurt and let down by people you love. I know it must feel like that's just the way it is, and it's scary to get close to people and feel hurt like that again. But I care about you, we care about you. I want you to know how it feels to be really close to someone you love, and feel safe, so we're going to make that happen."

6. **Promise you will address the original mode goal and care for the inner child.**

   Back to detached protector: "Look, just give us a trial. If you give me a little time, I can prove to you that we can let people in and still be safe."

   Say to your inner child: "Trust me, I'm going to help you see how much other people care about you and how you're worth it. You really deserve this, and I want you to feel better."

Example 2: Difficult Coping: Bully

Image prompt. Picture yourself super angry, red-faced, with a mean, contemptuous look. That should do it!

Background. The bully category of the the difficult coping mode is triggered after some kind of emotional hurt happens. It's basically the "a good offense is the best defense" strategy. For this exercise, let's imagine the bully was triggered when your best friend was trying to tell you that she really wishes you would not be so late when you meet. For whatever reason, it turns our you're always at least twenty minutes late when you get together, and she's saying she's kind of fed up. And your bully doesn't want to hear it.

Obviously, an important quality of the bully is the speed of it getting triggered. The triggering is usually very quick to happen and will take some practice managing. One way to do that is focus on anticipatory signals from your body (including rapid heart rate, pit in stomach, pressure on chest, shaking hands, flushed complexion). If you can learn to recognize the signal of that temper rising, you can intervene before you act. In other words, we are getting your brain involved before your mouth starts working. So with this exercise, imagine as the dialogue starts, you notice the feeling of your temper rising in your gut, or wherever else you tend to feel anger.

1. **Connect with the mode to get its attention.** "Okay, whoa, I know you're really triggered right now and very angry. You want to roar and burst out with your feelings right now. Try to hold on for just a second before anything happens. Let's just talk for a sec."

2. **Explain the mode's *goal* and validate in the context of unmet needs.** "Look, I know you are touchy about anyone criticizing you. Growing up, Little You only got criticism with no praise or affection. That really sucked, and you were stuck in a lousy situation. So you tried to protect yourself in the only way you could, which was to get angry. That was the only way anyone heard you! I would have done the same thing."

3. *Explain the harm* **this mode is causing.** "But let's fast-forward to the present. You know that Little You needed to yell and scream and attack to get heard, and it made sense then. But now, let's face it, when you hurt people this way, you have to admit, it makes you feel more alone, right?"

4. **Set a *limit* for the mode behavior.** "Now let's just hold on. I'm going to take it from here. You've been yelling and attacking as a way to protect Little You, but we don't need to do that anymore. I want to take care of Little You right now (takes their hand). You're not going to yell; you're not going to attack. I'm going to take care of this, explain what we need, and make sure Little You doesn't lose a friend. Now, before we go on, I have to ask you one thing: Is your friend right—are you late a lot? Can you see her point of view? How would you feel if your friend were twenty minutes late all the time? I know you! You would be angry about how valuable your time is. So maybe we can be more considerate?"

5. **Care for your inner child with compassion, validation, and soothing.** "Listen, I know maybe you feel better when the bully yells. It's like you're being heard, right? It feels like what you need. But I want you to get what you really need; that's attention and understanding. You love your friend, and I want her to hear how you feel and make it so you can get closer. We'll say we're sorry and try to explain."

6. ***Promise* you will address the original mode goal and care for your inner child**. "Your friend is really going to listen, I know it. I want to show you that you can feel heard and also feel love. Just give me a chance, I'll prove it!"

Dialogue with the Inner Critic Mode

Image prompt. As I've mentioned, your inner critic may be the voice of a parent or a harsh version of yourself and is demanding or punitive in tone. So pull together an image of someone, whether your parent or you, with a stern, perhaps harsh look on their face, maybe with arms akimbo or folded rigidly.

Background. As you know, the inner critic can take a more punitive or a demanding tone, often both. For this exercise, let's go with the punitive tone. Let's imagine you just got back from a first date. You're getting ready for bed and still feeling excited and hopeful about how it went, and you're going over the evening's events. Your inner critic is latching on to all the moments in the evening where you supposedly screwed up and telling you that you were terrible: "You don't deserve to be with anyone because you're so bad at this." And for good measure, it adds, "Even if it did go well, sooner or later they are going to see the real you, and things will fail."

1. **Connect with the mode to get its attention.** "OH MY GOD, SHUT UP! I am not going to stand for this. You absolutely cannot talk to me that way. If I heard you talking to someone else that way, I would say you are a total asshole. No one deserves that."

   (Until now, you've seen that I used a very measured, understanding tone with the coping child and difficult coping modes. We always want to make peace with the modes and connect with them. But in the case of the inner critic, depending on how mean it is, it's more effective to respond with anger—not to mention, more appropriate! It's what's needed to get the mode's attention. Anger at its core is about self-care. Once you have more control, you can use a more compassionate approach with the inner critic, but the initial anger with the inner critic is a key phase of recovery.)

2. **Explain the mode's *goal* and validate in the context of unmet needs.** "I get that you are trying to help Little You. You felt totally on your own growing up, the stakes were high, and it felt like if you messed up, bad things would happen. So you had to do it on your own and not mess up. You think Little You needs

you, and if you're not there, things will fall apart. At this point, it seems like you also don't have faith that Little You can manage at all without you."

3. **Explain *the harm* this mode is causing.** "The problem is, you perpetuate this idea that Adult You can't succeed without you being mean. I suppose you think, *Unless I'm mean, I won't be heard.* The truth is, when you act this way, you destroy Adult You's self-confidence, so Adult You has a harder time. The fact is, *you* are actually the problem now; *you* are making Adult You have less self-esteem. And it has to stop."

4. **Set a *limit* for the mode behavior.** "If you want to have ambition and high standards, no problem, I'm with that. But no more meanness, no more undermining, no more abuse. You're making Little You believe that they are no good, and that is unacceptable. Next time this happens, I'll be all over you again!"

5. **Care for your inner child with compassion, validation, and soothing.** "Come on, let's go. I don't want you to listen to that meany. You are good just the way you are. You are beautiful just the way you are. I want you to feel good about yourself— just like how I feel good about you. We all have things to work on and room for growth; that's normal. You are great, and I want to share you with the world! I want you to trust that I can take care of you and make sure you do well in the world. I want people to see you at your confident best, which is the real you!"

6. **Promise you will address the original mode goal and care for your inner child.** "You have nothing to lose here. I'm going to show you that we can feel good about you and have confidence

and that good things will happen. You're really great, and I'm going to make sure other people see that. And it's going to feel good."

After reading the examples, I'm sure you have an idea of one or two or more modes you would like to work with—just remember to use the "Mode Chart" you completed in chapter 4, based on the mode portraits in that chapter.

Exercise: Mode Dialogue Practice

I'd like you to set about thirty minutes aside in a private space where you won't be disturbed. You are going to arrange three chairs using a chair-work technique to represent your "Theater of Your Personality Mode Map" diagram in real life. You'll number the chairs, 1, 2, and 3. Arrange the three chairs like this: chair 1 and chair 2 are facing each other, and chair 3 is behind chair 2. You are going to sit in chair number 1.

You are sitting in the chair of your healthy caring adult, and you're facing your difficult mode (coping child, difficult coping, or inner critic) in the chair across from you. In the chair behind the mode is your inner child. So it looks like this:

Chair 1 = healthy caring adult (facing chair 2)

Chair 2 = difficult mode (facing chair 1)

Chair 3 = inner child (behind chair 2, facing the back of the difficult mode's chair)

If you can set up chairs in a private space and act out the scene, that's preferable. If that's not possible, you can use your imagination and make this a journaling exercise.

When you're ready to start the exercise, I suggest having a voice recorder app on your phone ready to record (Behary 2019). You can use the recording later to write down some key moments for a flashcard (explained later in this chapter). It may feel a little funny at first recording this, but don't worry, you'll get used to it and find it helpful. Maybe even start by trying to have fun with it.

Just like the examples above, you will complete your own dialogue using the "Mode Dialogue Practice Sheet," which is available at http://www. newharbinger.com/50997. If you aren't using the worksheet, just copy the prompts below into your journal. You'll want to keep completed copies in your journal.

The main goal of this exercise is to practice being your healthy caring adult, but you'll also practice speaking in the other modes. I want you to feel a sense of ownership over this process, practice in ways you're comfortable with, as well as stretch outside your comfort zone when you can. The goal is for you to speak out loud in each of the roles and to move into the appropriate chair for each role in the scene. Based on my clinical experience, I can tell you, it really makes a difference to sit in the different chairs! But again, do what you are comfortable with. I would rather you do this in a way that works for you, than not do it at all due to feeling pressure to do it "right."

Decide on a background story to work with—one that involves a tough situation triggered by a mode. This should come from a problem you're currently dealing with—a trigger that happens in a certain relationship, a procrastination, or a mood issue.

Start in the healthy caring adult chair, and you will see the mode in the chair across from you and the inner child behind them. The way the chairs are arranged will help you stay focused on the goal of this exercise (or the scene's plot): the healthy caring adult is dealing with the difficult mode in order to reach the inner child and take care of them with care and compassion. Use the worksheet or the prompts below to guide you through the dialogue process.

This practice may be intimidating at first, but it's pretty simple. You're sitting across from a difficult mode (coping child, difficult coping, or inner critic), seeing your inner child behind them, and you use your six principles to talk to them. You'll do fine!

First, on the worksheet or in your journal, write your answers to the following prompts:

1. Briefly describe the behavior, mood, or mindset you would like to address with your healthy caring adult. You may notice this mindset getting triggered at work, in relationships, or when spending time alone. What schemas and modes are triggered? Write down the setting, context, and events around the triggering.

2. Select a mode: coping child, difficult coping, or inner critic. Briefly describe the mode, for example its appearance and body language.

3. Describe your inner child, for example their age, appearance, and behavior.

The Six Principles of Mode Dialogue Script

When you are ready to begin the dialogue, use the following prompts to guide your verbal dialogue (or your written responses, if you're choosing to do write out the dialogue). Remember, you're starting with the healthy caring adult.

1. *Connect* with the mode and get its attention.

   • Healthy caring adult says to mode:

   • Mode's response:

   • Healthy caring adult's reaction:

2. Explain the mode's *goal* and validate in the context of unmet needs.

   • Healthy caring adult says to mode:

   • Mode's response:

   • Healthy caring adult's reaction:

3. *Explain* the harm this mode is causing.

   - Healthy caring adult says to mode:

   - Mode's response:

   - Healthy caring adult's reaction:

4. Set a *limit* for the mode behavior.

   - Healthy caring adult says to mode:

   - Mode's response:

   - Healthy caring adult's reaction:

5. *Care* for the inner child with compassion, validation, and soothing.

   - Healthy caring adult says to mode:

   - Mode's response:

   - Healthy caring adult's reaction:

6. *Promise* you will address the original mode goal and care for the inner child.

   - Healthy caring adult says to mode:

   - Mode's response:

   - Healthy caring adult's reaction:

Nurturing the Connection Between Your Inner Child and Healthy Caring Adult

Your North Star throughout this process is the caring relationship you build between your healthy caring adult and your inner child. The crucial point is that your healthy caring adult is able to take action in your adult world to care for your needs in ways the child was never able to access in the child world. It comes down to the independence and power you, as an adult, hold for your own destiny, while child-you, by definition, had to rely fully on adults. That's exactly why difficult modes develop: to cope with that dependency and caregiver failure in tough situations.

So as you go through the process of managing your modes using the six principles of dialogue, keep in mind the overall goal of mode dialogue: to build a bond between your inner child and your healthy caring adult. Now, I want to share some best practices to help manage your approach and expectations. You can think of these best practices as values and guidance.

Like Learning an Instrument

You are developing new perspectives on yourself and others, and this takes time. This may be the most important point to keep in mind. You are cultivating new ways of experiencing emotion, pain, and compassion. Most of us are so accustomed to learning a new idea and imagining we can take it into our way of being just like that. But building a sensitivity to the relationship between your inner child and healthy adult is a practice, like learning an instrument more than remembering an idea. It's experiential and takes practice to improve. You are bringing out parts of yourself that have been veiled your whole life or are entirely new to you. It'll take some time before these parts of yourself can reliably be activated and help you make real change in your life. Using the six-step mode dialogue practice format, I want you to practice. Try working with more than one triggering event and even different modes.

Generosity and Acceptance

By opening up to your inner child, you're letting in memories, current experiences of scary feelings, and vulnerability that can be overwhelming at times. As you open up to more vulnerability, you will also be wrangling those tough modes, which will demand a parental kind of tolerance and fortitude. You'll need to keep coming back to the principles of treating yourself with acceptance and generosity, which will help you avoid getting stuck in conflict with yourself.

Power

As you stay open to noticing your inner child, remember the primary difference between coping child reactions and healthy adult reactions is *power*. Children are, by definition, dependent on adults for care, surviving, and thriving. Children don't have the power to maintain and cultivate their boundaries and destinies. Obviously, this changes over time, but we all start from the same place of dependency. Our modes develop in childhood precisely as a way of working around our lack of power. If we can't say "no" or say what we need, we must do our best to work around the scenario and cope. Our healthy caring adult mode has agency and the power to self-advocate and can demonstrate to our coping child mode that things are different now. So when you are trying to understand a reaction, ask yourself whether the reaction is about feeling powerless. If it is, then it's likely to be a coping child, difficult coping, or inner critic mode. You can then ask yourself how to handle it differently if you had the power of an adult. Because, hey, you do now!

Exercise: Mode Image Diary and Mode Flashcard

The "Mode Image Diary" and "Mode Flashcard" are two common CBT and schema therapy exercises that I adapted and combined here into a two-part exercise that you can use every day. (Both worksheets are available for download at http://www.newharbinger.com/50997.)

The first exercise, "Mode Image Diary," helps you track when a tough mode is triggered and then practice managing the experience of being triggered with your healthy caring adult. Then you transform the results of your mode image diary into a mode flashcard—on which you'll distill and simplify your healthy message to your troublesome modes. The flashcard helps make mode dialogue as easy as possible to use in the moment. Collect the flashcards in your journal and keep them in your phone as handy way to coach yourself with mode management.

Part 1: Mode Image Diary

In the mode image diary, which you complete anytime a difficult mode is triggered, you start by describing the incident that triggered you (question 1 in the left column). You keep a picture of this incident in your mind's eye as you do this exercise, hence the "image" part of the image diary. Next, identify the particular mode that was triggered (question 2 in the left column). Then, you engage that mode (question 3 in the left column) using the first four of the six principles you learned: connect, goal, explain the harm, and limit. After that, you connect with your inner child (questions 4 and 5 in the left column), using principles five and six: care and promise. Ultimately, the diary is a simple way of catching on paper how you engage with your modes in daily life so you can easily be more self-aware, which improves with practice.

Mode Image Diary Questions	Six Healthy Caring Adult Principles	Your Answers
1. Trigger: 2. Mode triggered: 3. Healthy caring adult's response to mode:	• Connect • Goal • Explain the harm • Limit	
4. Where is your inner child, and what are they feeling? 5. Healthy caring adult's care for and validation of inner child's feelings:	• Care • Promise	

This is a way of practicing the mode dialogue interventions outlined above in the six principles of mode dialogue.

Mode Image Diary People Study

Let's do an example with a people study so it's easier to visualize. This time, we'll work with Ze and a scene from a day in their life.

Recall that Ze has the mistrust/abuse schema, among others, and that their angry child gets very active in response to being hurt and neglected. But Ze holds in that anger and often resorts to a compliant surrender form of the difficult coping mode as a way of outwardly coping.

Ze works as an organizer on trans rights, and recently, after Ze gave a presentation on outreach strategy at a meeting with a group of collaborating organizations, someone representing a faith-based homeless services group, who was clearly showing resistance to inclusiveness around trans rights, challenged Ze on whether people "need to be singled out by gender."

Ze tried to make an argument that validating gender identity would influence the reputation of their work in good ways. Ze wasn't sure the speaker was even listening. To top it off, this person used the wrong pronouns for Ze twice. Ze corrected him, which added tension in the room. While Ze felt that they had been assertive, made a good argument, and represented themself well, they carried a heavy feeling of fatigue and frustration for the rest of the day. Later, Ze caught themself dreading going home to their partner. On the train home, Ze wrote out a mode image diary on their phone.

1. Trigger: *Shitty meeting made me frustrated, and now I just want to be alone!*

2. Mode triggered: *Angry child*

3. Healthy caring adult's response to mode: *I felt you upset since the end of that meeting. I know it really made you angry, and you hate that guy now, right? You just wanted to scream at him, so he never bothers anyone like this again. But we're going home now, you're in a grumpy mood, and your partner doesn't deserve that. So try to cool out a little bit. It's over. Adult Ze was good and handled him well. It's good.*

4. Where is your inner child, and what they are feeling? *I felt attacked by that guy, like he was trying to tear apart what I do, the relationships that I built, and the people I love. He doesn't get it. It feels like he's part of the problem. I felt just like I did in my family, hurt and alone—and right in front of everyone too! I felt like I would never be safe.*

5. Healthy caring adult's care for and validation of inner child's feelings: *I know you felt really attacked by this guy. That really stinks. I would feel that way too. But you deserve never to feel that way. No one should have to feel that way, especially in a place that's supposed to feel safe. But I want you to remember that I was there for you. He's going to come away from that meeting really thinking about what he did. I know it. I stood up for you and made sure he understood how he sounds and that he needs to expand*

his outlook. And I don't think he's going to mess up your pronouns again; although if he does, I'll help us take it up the chain to higher management, so we can advocate for ourselves. We can do that now. We know that people do mess this up, and it may happen again. If so, I'll have your back. Now don't you want to go home and get in the arms of your partner and feel good instead of grumpy and alone?

You can see in the above example that Ze was able to connect with the angry child, explain that they understood what the angry child wanted, explain the harm, and set a limit. Then Ze went on to let the inner child express themself and offer a reminder that the healthy caring adult actually did a good job! I think by the time Ze got home after doing the flashcard (below), they were able to have a good evening. And as part of a longer-term goal, Ze took another step in overcoming the inclination to isolate after triggering.

Now try practicing a mode image diary yourself. Remember, this exercise is a diary entry based on a real event that triggered you, grounded in the image of a real memory. Put the five questions on paper (or download the worksheet available at http://www.newharbinger.com/50997) or type them into a note on your phone, and practice going through them with one of your difficult modes. I'm sure you already have an idea of a mood or behavior you would like to change. Practice filling in the questions and try reading the dialogue out loud or even into a voice-memo recording. Then, go through the same process the next time you find a mode of yours triggered in your day-to-day life. It may feel a bit awkward at first, but you'll get the hang of it, and I think you'll see how useful and effective it will be.

Part 2: Mode Flashcard

In this section you'll create a flashcard that captures the "greatest hits" of your healthy caring adult talking to your modes. You want to capture the most effective things your healthy caring adult says in the chair-work practice (the "Mode Dialogue Practice" exercise) so in the future, you can quickly remember them and easily refer to them.

Let's say Ze has the angry child, compliant surrender, detached protector, and punitive inner critic modes. As Ze does the mode image diary and flashcards for each of these modes over time, they build useful experience they can call on to manage mode dialogue. The flashcard, just like one for a math class, just makes the mode dialogue process easier.

Once you complete a mode image diary entry, if you feel it was particularly helpful and a "keeper," then put what you said to your tough mode in step 3 on a flashcard. Similarly, you can create flashcards from step 5 of your mode image diary, boiling down the most effective ways that your healthy caring adult soothes your inner child in many different contexts. You may want to take out some detail specific to an event and hold on to the helpful words.

Here's a flashcard Ze might develop from the above scene:

Mode: *Angry child*

What your healthy caring adult says: *I felt you upset. I know it really made you angry right? But we're going home now, you're in a grumpy mood, and your partner doesn't deserve that. So I'm going to need you to cool out a little bit. It's over. Adult Ze was good and handled him well. It's good.*

Once you start practicing the mode image diary and coming up with flashcards yourself, these flashcards could also go in your phone, perhaps in separate folders titled "Angry Child," "Compliant Surrender," and whatever other labels are appropriate. When you are feeling triggered, you can just scroll through what will become a collection of encouraging words your healthy caring adult has said to you. You can also keep these statements as voice memos that you can play back to yourself. And you can update the language on your flashcards in your journal and elsewhere as your dynamic with your modes and the particular ways you relate to them (and they relate to you) change over time.

The Upward Cycle of Behavior Change

Now you're going to take the skills you just learned and work out how you use them to make sustained behavior change in your daily life and grow as a person.

At this stage of your experience with this book, I hope you're seeing the value these tools offer for making real change in your life—in daily life but also in who you are. Using your mode image diary, you'll notice all the moments in your day when tough modes tell you what to do; using your flash cards, you'll have easy ways to intervene and make different choices. This all adds up to profound change over the long term. Having the self-confidence to leave a job or start dating are huge examples. Mode dialogues and your healthy caring adult can help you overcome self-sabotage in the creative process, build more confidence in relationships at work and in your personal life, finally express your needs and anger in productive ways, feel more attunement with your emotions and less detached, and even overcome some problematic habits holding you back.

So behavior change is a key element of the schema therapy approach and ultimately the goal of this whole process! After all, if I can't help you change your behavior, I'm not helping you change your problematic ways of coping. But beyond the obvious, behavior change plays a special role as an engine that drives an upward cycle or spiral of change.

In your use of schema therapy to change coping styles, you'll see that working on behavior change becomes an important method for staying engaged with your modes by pushing yourself outside your comfort zone. This is the positive, upward cycle of the schema therapy approach: each time you move outside your comfort zone with experience, you trigger a mode and another opportunity to engage with your healthy caring adult mode. And with each new chance to get outside your comfort zone, you are pushing the limits of your resilience and tolerance of stress and getting closer to your behavior change goals.

Behavior-Change Formula

I have a simple four-step formula for you to move into your own upward cycle. You'll be using the "Mode Image Diary" and "Mode Flashcard" exercises to change your behavior with these four steps. Think of these skills as a way to metabolize your stuckness and make change happen through self-dialogue.

1. *Identify a difficult behavior or habit* you want to change and label which mode is behind it. For example, "I don't want to take naps during the day, and my detached self-soother disagrees!"

2. *Picture an alternative action* in line with your healthy caring adult values to replace the difficult behavior. "When I feel the temptation to lie down, I'm going to go for a walk and do five minutes of mindfulness with my healthy caring adult."

3. Now do a *mode image diary entry* using a dialogue between your healthy caring adult, the tough mode, and your inner child around making this behavior change. "I know my detached self-soother wants me to nap as a way of avoiding my work anxiety, so I will talk to them and address the anxiety directly."

4. Create a *mode flashcard* with talking points from the healthy caring adult to speak directly to the anxiety and reassure your inner child. Put the text in your journal or record a voice-memo in your phone. "I know it's a relief to fall asleep and escape, but it just makes you feel worse. We can take this on in a way that makes you feel better about yourself. You don't have to feel anxious, I got you."

Try working with these steps for the next week or two. See if using your mode image diary and flashcards to shape your self-talk, plant the seeds for behavior change, and make the change itself easier do and to stick to. Feel free to journal about the benefits you might be seeing or the roadblocks or obstacles that might arise. Slowly, as you continue working with the tools you've learned in this chapter, the process of change will become easier. You'll notice it's easier and easier to act from the position of your healthy caring adult self, rather than being driven by your modes and your old ways of coping. And in the process, the inner child within you will find its needs are met, rather than suppressed. And you'll be increasingly able to live the life you want to live.

Moving Forward

This chapter had a lot of moving parts, but once you practice the "Mode Image Diary" and "Flashcard" exercises and add them to your journal, you'll see that it's an intuitive practice for two things: having a productive, compassionate dialogue with yourself, and tracking your progress. At the end of the day, the essence of this practice is nurturing the relationship between your inner child and your healthy caring adult. This is a bit like learning a musical instrument: at first it may feel clunky, but after a few weeks, it will come easily.

Chapter 7

Becoming the New You: Mindfulness and the Ecosystem of Growth

At this point in our journey together, you've accomplished quite a lot, right? You made a connection with Little You, which became a vision of your inner child. You learned about your schemas and triggers. You learned which modes you use to manage your schemas and how those modes impact your life. You also learned about your healthy caring adult, how to cultivate it, and how to use your healthy caring adult to manage your modes. You also got some tips on how to use a behavior-change formula to keep momentum going in a positive direction.

At this stage, hopefully you feel more confident with your mode-dialogue skills, more comfortable with your inner child, and more enthusiastic about your healthy caring adult mode. You may even have developed exciting challenges for yourself about your values and identity.

You may be wondering how a question as huge as identity comes into the picture of just changing coping skills. But consider how the progression of change happens: it begins with small things in daily life and eventually moves to big questions of who you are. Small behavior changes lead to changes in mindset, self-awareness, and a sense of what's possible, and once you have different beliefs about what's possible, you naturally start to see yourself differently. Here's an example of what I mean. If you once saw yourself as socially awkward—maybe due to poor support as a child and a strong inner critic—and you overcome those self-criticisms, then don't you become someone who is no longer socially awkward? What kinds of doors open to you in areas of dating, love, social life, and career? Now you're considering possibilities that were never before in your mind. That means a new you!

That's the crux of my argument for why this book should come before any other self-help book. If you are looking at making improvements in your life, you want to start with as little interference from your coping child, difficult coping, and inner critic modes as possible, right? All else comes after that. Otherwise, all the modes are grinding gears.

This chapter offers suggestions for answering the questions that arise once the modes that have been a big influence all your life start to fade. I'll offer ways to navigate the experience of transforming into the person you want to be.

You're going to focus on gaining clarity on the big directions you want to focus on in life to complement the smaller day-to-day changes that you've begun to implement. You'll work to list some bold goals for change, the major milestones you want to hit in your life. You'll ask and answer exciting questions such as: "What if I got out of my own way and nothing was stopping me? Who would I want to be?" You'll explore what it's like to be you when your modes are no longer in charge.

Ecosystem of Growth

One of the most powerful elements of human experience is habit. Whether good or bad, habits are essentially routines and practices that become a part of who we are at a subconscious level. You could say that modes are the most ingrained habit we have, becoming part of who we are over the course of our lives. That's why, when you change your modes, you are also changing who you are.

It's also true that our various habits interlock with each other to form our larger patterns of behavior. In the last chapter, I talked about the upward cycle of behavior change. Over time, the upward spiral of change, when it's aided and maintained through consistent daily practice with your mode image diary, flashcards, and the other ways you structure your adaptive self-talk and behavior change—your day-to-day habits—manifests a still-larger pattern that I call an ecosystem of growth.

The goal of setting up an ecosystem of growth is to set in place a series of habits that support each other and incorporate the new parts of you as you discover them. This is a kind of "set it and forget it" evolution of the self: as long as you trust the ecosystem and the work you've done to engineer and cultivate it, your growth will happen—and with success comes deeper change.

Here's an example of what I mean. Say you start with a detached self-soothing behavior such as doomscrolling. You introduce a smaller scale behavior-change goal, like taking fifteen minutes in your day for mindfulness meditation or maybe ten minutes of journaling on your inner child and how to care for them. Over two weeks, your online detaching transitions into a more self-caring behavior. Your mind opens up to new activities as a result, like reading poetry or raising houseplants as a hobby. Your mindset becomes kinder and more compassionate; you become more self-confident. As the weeks pass, you find that since you're detached so much less, you have hours of spare time in your week to get involved in new activities and life pursuits. It's like someone gave you more spare time!

Now, you might be asking yourself: "How will I use this time? Am I the kind of person who runs a book club? Am I someone who could write a novel? Can I really go back to school? Could I turn my houseplant hobby into a blog community?" To accommodate all these new questions about yourself, you'll need a ritual to stop to appreciate the change you made and recalibrate for more ambitious goals, whether personal, work, social, or spiritual.

When it comes to orchestrating an ecosystem of growth, you can break this process down into six phases (some of which you'll already be familiar with), which cycle and repeat. These phases are:

Behavior-change goals

Planner

Mindfulness

Journal

Self-retreat

Revised life goals

The pivot point in this model is when the last step flips back to the first one, when the small behavior-change goals you've achieved tell you when to update your larger life goals, in other words, as your sense of who you are evolves. This is when you can see the smaller, daily change you're making turn into big implications for your life. You're going from merely coping with what arises to actively shaping the direction of your life. This broad awareness inspires you with the smaller, daily change you continue to make.

When your efforts to change begin to yield an ecosystem of growth, you'll take smaller behavior change more seriously, since you can see how it fits into a bigger picture. Another benefit of valuing small change as part of large change is that you feel small change is less high stakes. High-stakes thinking makes you more prone to disappointment, frustration, and giving up. On the contrary, when you see small change as a piece of the process of much larger change, you'll have more patience with it. You'll see the long game. That patience will give you more strength to continue. Now let's take a closer look at the phases of the ecosystem of growth.

Behavior-Change Goals

Remember these simple steps for changing a particular behavior or pattern: select the behavior you want to change, think of an alternative action to replace it, and do an entry in your mode image diary around what you experience with the behavior. Then create a flashcard with a quick solution to have on hand and use in the moment, whenever you need to. You could think of this practice as a kind of behavior-change machine you can switch on.

Now, as a practice, this can be highly effective. But the trick is to hold the motivation to do it, to remember to do it, and to not forget doing it over and over until you hit your goal. In this sense, repetition is important, and in early experience, you are moving uphill against the power of an old habit, which tells you over and over, "Just do it the old way; it feels better!" So how to overcome this habit energy and stay motivated?

It comes down to having and using one tool: a planner.

Planner

This is your secret weapon, your box of tricks, utility belt, magic spells—however you want to put it. The strategy is simple, and you may already use it in your daily life. You schedule activities in your planner and then sync your planner with the calendar on your phone so any event in your planner will have a notification or alert connected to it to remind you to do it. For the system to work, you must pair that calendar function with an alert. The alert is the sensory "ping" that will get you to actually do what you've scheduled.

Ultimately, your planner, when paired with your smartphone calendar (with notification alerts), will work as another "set it and forget it" device in your daily life. You may be wondering, *Instead of an analog planner, can't I just use the calendar on my phone?* I suggest an analog planner, at least until you've mastered this process, because it has the feel of a journal, and you can look at your full day or week with pen in hand and take notes on successes and challenges. You'll want to schedule two types of appointments in your calendar: building-block and interceptor.

BUILDING-BLOCK APPOINTMENTS

You can use the building block to introduce new positive habits into your life, the kind that, when done over time, will help you achieve large-scale goals—such as meditation, working out, or engaging in a creative activity that you might want to do but also find intimidating, like writing or music. You can also use building-block appointments to set aside time to give your healthy caring adult a chance to check in with all your modes or to check in with your journal and pull out any flashcards you may find handy to work with that day.

Block out as much time as you think you need to accomplish your building-block task. Obviously, how you schedule depends on what you schedule: meditation may be fifteen minutes every morning, while writing a novel may be two hours a day or doing a hike is twice monthly. Just think about what makes sense for frequency of the activities. Make sure there are no scheduling conflicts. You can also include more abstract items like "journal time" or "review flashcard time." Also—and this is very important—set up an alert or notification in your phone to go along with this calendar item. If you rely on a planner to organize your life, you know that having a regular self-check to review your schedule and make any adjustments is an excellent practice to feel in control of your time. So the recurring appointment in your schedule is your new best friend.

INTERCEPTOR APPOINTMENTS

Interceptor appointments allow you to focus on smaller-scale interventions for difficult behaviors as a set of short-term and one-off steps. Let's say you know you have a job interview coming up and suffer from imposter syndrome (a loud inner critic mode), you have a meeting with your boss, and you know your angry child will get triggered, or you have a date and want to avoid being a people-pleaser (self-sacrifice schema). Add a fifteen- or thirty-minute interceptor appointment to your schedule just before these events so you can focus on a flashcard to manage the schema and mode and practice being in the situation as a healthy caring adult. You're "intercepting" the mode-triggering with a good talk from your healthy caring adult. Think about other activities in your life that are difficult, that bring your less-adaptive modes to the fore—such as joining a 12-step group or working on your online dating profile—and imagine intercepting that discomfort so you're better placed to overcome it.

WORKING WITH YOUR PLANNER GOING FORWARD

The main challenges of using a planner go in a couple of directions. First, you ignore your notifications—the tools meant to help you actually do what you set out in your planner. Second, you end up overplanning and demanding too much of yourself. And the system breaks down.

We've all been there. You set up a notification for a new routine you want to include in your life, like working out, and soon, when the notification goes off, you just swipe it away and ignore it. You've developed the dark art of ignoring your planner! You might think I have a life hack for you right now. Not really. When we start ignoring our best intentions as they manifest in the form of a reminder notification, we (being good students of schema therapy) know a difficult mode is at work, right? So no, I can't help you magically respond to all of your notifications in the moment. Rather, how can you talk back to the mode that takes over and prevents you from doing what you need to do? Now we come back to your mode diary and your flashcard tools. Talk to the rebellious child who gets a thrill from swiping away reminders or talk to your protector who is keeping you from the pain and vulnerability of trying. You can do it!

Ultimately, the more you see using your planner as part of a process, rather than something you're "either good or bad at," the more likely you are to succeed over time—as long as you don't give up. So manage your expectations before starting and be okay with some ups and downs in the process. You'll find your own rhythm and style. When you introduce a new behavior into your life, expect at least two weeks of ups and downs with it at first.

Also, know that your modes are cunning and always, always paying attention! You may believe that your healthy caring adult is going to set up a plan to work out more often. Next thing you know, an alarm is going off every day at 5:00 a.m. and you are bullying yourself into working out for ninety minutes a day. That demanding inner critic has snuck into your planning! Your unrelenting standards are a pressure telling you to ask for more. And then you may react with anger. "This sucks. I am not someone who works out!" It's not uncommon at all for people to have a war going on between their inner critic and an angry or rebellious child, and it takes practice to develop a healthy caring adult who can rise above and mediate. So if you notice you are demanding too much of yourself and it's making you angry, stay cool and do a mode image diary. Use your mode diary to guide yourself to accept your anger and care for it, tempering the demanding tone, tolerating the idea that "you could do more," and being comfortable with starting small to plant a seed of change that will eventually grow durable and flourish in your ecosystem. In the end, the more aware you are of this dynamic, the more you can overcome it.

Mindfulness

Mindfulness—the ability to pay nonjudgmental attention to all aspects of your bodily, thought, and emotional experience in a given moment—is a key ingredient in this formula of self-evolution. Mindful attention to your own experience in day-to-day life will help you connect the principles of the healthy caring adult with your own life values. As you work with your modes in ways large and small, mindfulness practice will open up new coping skills in everyday life. You could say that mindfulness is the fuel that keeps the change machine going. A daily mindfulness practice will make you feel better in the moment and give you the self-compassion and patience to move toward larger life goals. Over time, it will help you metabolize who you are: your values will inform your choices, and your actions will tell you more about your values, in a repetitive flow.

When you hear the word "mindfulness," what do you think about? It's common to view mindfulness as a kind of deep breathing practice, possibly with the idea of stopping your thoughts and "just being." If you have been less interested in mindfulness or think it's not for you, I'd like you to keep an open mind about it right now—be open to letting it in. I have found it to be an indispensable tool to use in work with coping skills, schemas, and modes.

MINDFULNESS FAQ

What is mindfulness? Mindfulness is the skill of focusing your attention, sometimes on your thoughts, sometimes on emotions, sometimes on body sensations, sometimes on sensory input like sounds or tastes, and sometimes on all of these. Here, we're going to start with the more formal practice of mindful meditation, which over time and with practice will build to include a less formal practice of being able to have mindful awareness while in the middle of other activities. Once you practice mediation, you will be able to use mindful awareness to manage modes, a key goal of the practice.

How do I do mindfulness meditation? Mindfulness meditation, as we'll do it here, is when you work on focusing your attention while either sitting or walking (Nhat Hanh 2010, 35–51). Here's a sketch of what's involved. I'll get into more detail in a minute:

You begin by drawing your attention inward and focusing on your breathing. You may take some deep breaths to begin, first focusing on your in-breath, then on your out-breath, the sound the breath makes, the experience of your chest filling and emptying of air, and the flow of air in your throat.

You may then focus on points of contact between your body and the earth: the soles of your feet, your legs, and your bottom while sitting or the sensation of your feet as they take turns touching the ground while walking.

Once you get going with these steps, you can then turn to focusing on all the different ways of adjusting your attention. I would suggest doing this practice for around ten minutes several days a week, or more if you like.

When you're getting started, think about it like learning an instrument, but one that you can play pretty well within just a few weeks. You'll need to get some of the basics down, a bit like learning your scales as a musician, before doing some of the mindful work with your modes.

Try to put a time in your planner when you are most likely to do it. You may have more luck starting your day with it because when you're just starting out, if you get caught up in your day, it's harder to change gears and meditate. (That will change once you get used to it.) I suggest blocking a total of fifteen minutes for meditation time, expecting to meditate for ten minutes of that time (you may actually be preparing for the meditation, gearing up, and winding down, during that fifteen-minute block). So start with getting settled and calm, and then see if you can do five minutes of meditation at first and just build up to the full ten minutes, with a few minutes for winding down post-meditation. Don't force it.

If you find that you get restless trying to sit for meditation (I raise my hand here!), then you can practice walking meditation using the same principles. You want to walk in a safe area, safe from traffic, on a route that doesn't demand too much attention. As you focus on the sound of your breathing and the body sensation of lifting each foot and leg and putting it down, you are using the same mindfulness practice with your thoughts.

It can also be helpful to fit your practice into a regular routine you already have. Attach it to another activity you do every day, say, just after you put your clothes on for the day before you leave for work. Just start with these simple steps; you can even do it right now:

- Give yourself three minutes on a timer. Sit in a comfortable position with your back straight and soles of your feet flat on the ground. Start the timer.

- With your eyes closed or just focused on a distant spot, draw your attention inward and notice your breathing.

- Without forcing yourself to breath outside of your regular rhythm, start following your inhales and exhales. You can even silently say to yourself "inhale" and "exhale" with each movement.

- As you focus on your breathing, you'll start to notice thoughts coming and going or that you're distracted from your focus; that's okay, just return your attention to your breath.

You'll notice the back-and-forth of how your attention drifts away from focusing on breathing to distracting thoughts and back again. That's good! That is the essential rhythm of the experience, and if you've been doing it for months or years, you'll still have that experience. You can build a wonderful practice on awareness of that back-and-forth.

MINDFULNESS AND THE HEALTHY CARING ADULT

As you develop a new grounded sensitivity to strong emotions and physical sensations, you'll become more aware of the calm place from which you notice difficult experiences. In other words, you're going to develop a grounded, calm, and patient baseline perspective. This is your mindful home for your healthy caring adult. Like the state of mindfulness itself, your healthy caring adult mind is already there for you as soon as you start trying. You reach your destination as soon as you start traveling toward it. So you can think of mindfulness itself as bonding with your healthy caring adult with the values of compassion, generosity, patience, and grounded confidence: all the traits that help you manage difficult modes. In this respect, to be in a mindful state is to be in the zone of healthy self-talk that schema therapy is all about. That's why mindfulness is so helpful. It's a regular practice that you do to build both a healthy baseline and a particular state of mind, a tool that you can use when you need it. If you get triggered, upset, or overwhelmed, call on mindfulness in the moment to connect with the healthy caring adult who may feel far away.

When you're feeling triggered—meaning hurt, angry, vulnerable, or in pain—you need a healthy caring adult who is welcoming, soothing, and supportive but who is also connected with a feeling and tone of love and joy. After all, your healthy caring adult is showing your modes a way to be fulfilled, safe, and happy, so you want your vision of healthy caring to include joy! In my own practice, I have found it crucial to feel linked with a sense of belonging to something larger than myself and to something that is joyous. So I suggest these key elements of a healthy caring adult and mindfulness practice.

Some Western approaches to mindfulness focus on certain aspects of the practices taught in Buddhism but remove the spiritual component. This is mindfulness as a means of treating symptoms or as a way of calming oneself, which are worthy goals. But in my experience, any approach to mindfulness that doesn't involve an element of joy, gratitude, positivity, and a vision of something bigger than yourself becomes a difficult and sometimes a technical, even grim pursuit. It's also true that whatever vision of joy, meaning, and connection you might choose to hold should be one you create based on your own needs, values, and direction—not someone else's idea of deeper meaning. So, you might opt to focus on the higher power or source in a religious tradition, or you might choose nature, the earth, or even more focused visions, such as music in all its forms, or love and compassion, as conscious pursuits in themselves.

Whatever spiritual vision you adopt should help you connect with:

- a sense of belonging to something larger than you

- a feeling of compassion for others and yourself

- joy, gratitude, and beauty.

If this is new territory for you, try to focus on little steps and don't force anything that doesn't feel authentic as part of who you are. You may want to go through a process of research and journaling on the topic to find what works for you. Above all, be open-minded about letting a new experience into your life. The spiritual element of mindfulness may be challenging for you, especially when you are just starting out getting some clarity between your healthy caring adult and your coping child, difficult coping, and inner critic modes. For example, the detached protector and inner critic often have a large influence on our healthy caring adult mode, and they can put a lot of chatter in your mind. The joy and kindness in mindful meditation can help you filter the noise—but it will take some time.

Once you have the beginnings of a nurturing, spiritual vision, you can fit it into your mindfulness practice as one of the regular steps you take. It may sound something like:

- "I remember the warmth and belonging I feel when I look at ocean waves or birds playing in the tree outside my window."

- "I am one part of this amazing blue planet moving through space, like a miracle."

- "I love the power and magic of music, how it moves me, how I am part of it."

- "I love how kind people were to each other on the commute this morning, and I am part of that kindness."

This will help you stay connected to playfulness, creativity, and authenticity, which adds an element of fulfillment to the mindfulness experience, keeping you engaged.

You will notice a different experience of yourself after a couple of weeks of regular mindfulness practice. You may feel in touch with your experience of breathing, be more sensitive to shifts in your emotions and stress, and generally be more aware of physical sensations. You may see the motivation behind mindfulness practice: this kind of sensitivity is incredibly helpful when it comes to noticing your emotional needs, mode thinking, and perspective on thoughts and feelings so you can make an intervention.

MINDFULNESS, EMOTIONAL NEEDS, AND YOUR INNER CHILD

By now, you may not find it surprising that people can avoid or detach from strong core emotions to such an extent that the emotions go unnoticed. As we've seen, this isn't really a "flaw" per se, but a way of coping. The problem is that the coping causes detachment and all the difficulty we've been addressing in this book. So regular mindfulness practice will help you notice strong feelings as they happen and overcome detachment. For example, you may notice feelings and be unsure of what triggered them. Pausing for a ten- or twenty-minute meditation can help you analyze what's happening. Such a meditation may be as simple as focusing on the in-breath and out-breath and saying to yourself, "I'm having difficult feelings—what may have happened?" and then, "I'm having difficult feelings; I will accept them and take care of them."

You can also use imagery work during a meditation, whether sitting or walking, to connect your difficult emotions to your inner child's core emotional needs. Since you're familiar with the unmet needs of Little You, it should be clear whether something in your day triggered them.

Let's come back to Judy as an example. Judy, you'll recall, grew up with an impatient mother who didn't allow for Little Judy's normal pace of learning new things and a father who was distant. She developed a painful defectiveness schema. Once day, in a meeting, a coworker rolled her eyes and said, "I guess we'll have to go through multiple rounds of checking and rechecking on this code." Judy felt like she had been punched in the gut and felt humiliated in front of the group but disguised her feelings. She knew she felt as though her coworker was saying the rounds of checking were due to Judy's own poor work. "They all think I make careless mistakes and hold the team back!" After the meeting, Judy was able to take a break and, because it was a nice day, go for a walking meditation.

Judy took her usual walking route so she wouldn't be distracted. She focused on her breathing. "I'm feeling hurt and rejected by what my colleague said. It feels like I was being told that I'm defective. I know this was a vulnerable child reaction." She then pulled an image of Little Judy into her mind and imagined walking with her. "Hi, little one! I'm so sorry this happened. I know sometimes your feelings get hurt, and it's not fair at all. There were a lot of times when your mom made you feel this way. It's never been your fault, and there isn't anything wrong with you. Your mom was impatient and didn't know what she was doing to you. You're a great little kid, who deserves to feel good about herself. And I'm always going to be right here to take care of you." Judy had done similar walking meditations on this route many times, and it had become a familiar safe place right in the middle of her workday.

Judy was also familiar enough with her defectiveness schema to know that it would have an effect of either making her sulk and become avoidant of the person who hurt her or making her accept and tolerate poor treatment from people without standing up for herself. Under the influence of her schema, Judy could walk away from this meeting believing that it is her fault that checking is required of the group work or wounded about the injustice of her colleague being mean.

But instead, Judy knew that through her dialogue between her healthy caring adult and Little Judy, she can validate her coping child mode's anger and act in response. That is, she can say something to her colleague, letting her know that what she said wasn't okay, and that it shouldn't happen again; Judy wasn't the only person working on this project, and her contribution shouldn't be singled out in such a way—a way that was simply rude and not constructive. Judy may also realize that her angry-child reaction was too much for the moment at hand. She could take a more low-key approach like, "Hey, that wasn't so nice when you said that, and it kind of stung. Could you avoid that next time?" She also knows that she can use mindfulness to let the feelings of the reactive, hurt child be there—without letting them drive her to sulk or internalize the feelings of being singled out or incapable the way she once did. And a mindful walk, using the tools within a meditation practice, helped her focus and be compassionate as she accomplished these steps.

A GUIDED MEDITATION TO CARE FOR MODES

You may approach coping with being triggered by noticing your schema and connecting with your inner child as I described above. But if you notice your triggering really has you stuck in a coping child, difficult coping, or inner critic mode, it may be too much to connect with the inner child, and the following mindful mediation approach to modes may work. This is a mediation based on the approach used by Thich Nhat Hanh and his followers in the Plum Village tradition as well as on elements of core mindfulness training by Tara Brach and Jack Kornfield.

This meditation will move you through a few phases designed to create a caring distance from a triggered mode. There are seven steps. If you would like, you can read these steps into a voice-memo app so you can listen to them as a guided meditation.

1. First, you will connect with your body, your posture, and the physical sensations of sitting or walking. You can sit in a mediation posture (in a chair or on the ground), relaxed and upright, with your spine straight and your hands resting in your lap, palms up. Focus on points of contact with the earth, whether the soles of your feet, your legs, or your bottom. Find a feeling of energy and magnetism with these points of contact and grounding.

2. Simply focus on the experience of your breath moving in and out as you let your thoughts pass in the background. Imagine your thoughts and their running commentary as a stream

running past you, flowing, but not distracting you. (Just do your best with this; you won't be perfect.) Focus on only your breath, even saying to yourself "in-breath" and "out-breath" as you breathe. Try this for about two minutes. Don't force yourself to breathe any particular way; just breathe as you need to.

3. Focus on sensory experience: What do you hear? What do you see? What do you feel on your skin—the temperature, your clothing, or perhaps a breeze? Are there any scents around you? Once you focus on each sensory input, try to take them all in at once. This will all help ground you.

4. Once you are grounded, reconnect with your vision of belonging and joy.

5. Return to a focus on what your tough mode is feeling, saying, and doing. You will repeat to yourself what your mode is saying and feeling.

6. Then picture your mode sitting or walking next to you, picturing yourself as separate from it; listen to the mode say how it feels and what it wants as you walk alongside.

7. Practice your healthy caring adult addressing the mode with compassion and love. "I know that you have taken care of me in the past, and now I will take care of you. I have a way of managing this that will help even more than what you're offering. Trust me and let me show you." If this becomes a longer dialogue, that's fine, as long as you are firm, set limits, and don't draw it out.

Feel free to use this as a template, substituting your own words as needed to make this feel like it's yours. And if you are successful, you can befriend your modes and more fully connect with your inner child. In that way, you move from the stress of modes to reconnecting with the joy, playfulness, and creativity of your inner child, which inspires you to do more!

Keeping the Ecosystem Healthy with a Journal, Self-Retreats, and Revising Life Goals

As you continue practicing your self-talk and your skills, your ecosystem of growth will continue to evolve, and in the weeks, months, and years to come, you can use your journal to reflect on and document the evolution you experience in your values and sense of identity as you go through the exciting process of change. From time to time, you'll want to take stock of the changes in your values that you're experiencing by having a self-retreat (phase 5) so you can deeply consider where you're going and what you want. During these self-retreats, you update your life goals (phase 6) and tweak your behavior change goals (phase 1) as a result, which gives you updated behavior-change goals to feed back into the beginning of the ecosystem cycle. So the whole cycle rolls over to the beginning as a renewal.

You may have come to this book thinking about how to stop the things that get in your way and keep you stuck. It's not uncommon to think, *Oh, I just have to stop doing this one bad behavior or stop this negative thought, and the rest will fall into place.* You may not even consider this section of the book a priority for that reason. But I want you to know that teaching yourself how to appreciate and cultivate your growth is key to being unstuck. You kind of don't have a choice! This isn't just about taking away problems (subtraction); it's also about building the habit of bringing good things into your mind (addition). You'll continue your healthy growth and evolution by doing both, and you will not be the same person you were when you started this journey.

So as you weave the healthy caring adult into your identity more and more, you'll use your healthy caring adult journal to document your journey of subtraction and addition and to tell you who you are becoming. As you program behavior change into your planner, build it into your life, and start to see results, you will document those results in your journal and tweak the process as you go, weekly or biweekly. At the end of the week, when you look at the results of your efforts, you'll see them through the eyes of your healthy caring adult (including the six principles of the healthy caring adult and the list of values you put together in chapter 5) and decide how to get better results next week. Mindfulness will also play a role: you'll view your efforts to change with self-acceptance, compassion, joy, and playfulness.

Your sense of self, values, and identity will change over time. Some of those changes will be noticeable on a weekly basis, like a potted plant; others will occur over a larger scale of time, perhaps months, like the seasons; and others will happen over years, like the climate. This larger scale of change over time will influence your sense of identity and likely have you revising life goals as you become more fully self-actualized.

Here's one more example of the six-phase process working. You start with an angry and emotional-deprivation schema, so you are quick to feel that you're being overlooked and neglected, which makes you lash out for the unfairness of it. This has left you feeling that you can only get so much out of relationships because people are not dependable. You start to track when these modes are triggered in your day and block in your planner some time to go over your mode dialogue. You begin to experience triggering moments from the healthy caring adult perspective and go for short meditation walks. You stop lashing out or being bitter with people. When you have meetings with your boss, you schedule an interception moment prior to the meeting to ground yourself. Over time, relationships change, and you open up to trusting people more. Your colleagues see you as more pleasant to work with and less bitter. Now you feel relief and have to ask yourself: "Am I really someone who likes people? If I like people, how much closer can I get to them?" Try having a self-retreat to explore what you've always wanted from relationships but thought wasn't possible until now.

Do you see the flow of change, of moving from daily, small interventions to large questions of next steps in life? I want to help you make sure you capture the potential in this change process and cultivate it. Self-retreats are a great way to do just that.

Quarterly Self-Retreat

Every ninety days or so, schedule a self-retreat. It doesn't need to be a big, exhaustive thing; it could be as little as an hour or so of your time. But it'll be dedicated time for you to take stock and reflect on what you've done over the last few months and on what you might like to do over the next few. You'll need your planner and your journal to review your recent work and experience with change. You may do this in a quiet, private place, wherever you find solace in the world. I suggest someplace special. This may be a local hiking trail, the beach, or your favorite spot in the local library. As you look over your journal, ask yourself, "Are the changes I'm making in line with what I value and how I want to treat myself?" This will help ensure difficult modes aren't slipping in. I strongly suggest adding a period of mindfulness to your retreat. So you'll do a review of the last three months, see what stands out for you, and then put aside twenty minutes or more for mindfulness, either sitting or walking. Then come back to your journal and document any insights you may have on the coming three-month period.

BIRTHDAY SELF-RETREAT LETTER TO YOURSELF

Every year on your birthday, give yourself a chance to check in from the perspective of your entire life story. You know how you hope for special plans on your birthday, that people you love will do something special for you? Hold that same attitude toward yourself too. Plan something special for yourself, which will involve a self-retreat on the big life-goal questions and where you want to go.

Imagine you are telling the story of your life to Little You, your inner child, up to the present day. You've been practicing caring for Little You for some time, and you're making progress becoming a better caregiver to yourself and listing to what your inner child needs. Now, you'll imagine the two of you looking into your future together. How do you want to close the loop of the pain, frustration, and hardship that Little You went through? Your time and your future are a gift, an opportunity for you to provide the goodness, safety, love, creativity, and accomplishment you've always yearned for—whatever that looks like for you. As an activity to share, sit down with Little You and compose a letter to your future self to be opened on your next birthday in one year. Give Little You a chance to say a few things and be sure to include words of encouragement and support, maybe some advice, as well as wishes for what you want to become. For the rest of the year, you'll have these words in the back of your mind as an inspiration.

Making Space for Future You

This brings us to the end of this book and our work together. But it's only the beginning of your work of making change for yourself. If you can continue the process of removing obstacles in your own life and mind and replacing them with opportunity and openness, you'll find ways of being you more creatively and being open to whatever might arise in the process.

I encourage you to stay open as you continue this work. It's not just about helping you validate your inner child but also about welcoming a future version of yourself, a version you don't know yet. Think about being a parent and whether you should tell your child what you expect them to be when they grow up. You can have wishes and hopes for your future-self as you continue to replace old modes and their unhelpful coping skills with the resources and capacities of your healthy caring adult. But you should also stay open to whatever might arise. In this way, the work of growth and creating new coping skills to replace ones that don't serve you is like any creative process. When you're creating something, whether it's writing a song or a novel, it always involves a compassionate acceptance for imperfection and flaws ("This is a draft and will get better") as well as openness to the unexpected ("This idea came from nowhere, and I love it"). The process of creating yourself involves the same openness. In the end, you're always a kind of draft version of yourself, a developing version of yourself, and to get closer to being the you who you want to be, you have to accept who you are with compassion and have confidence in your ability to welcome whoever you may become as you respond to the circumstances of life that shape you and that you shape in turn.

So, as we approach the end of this book, try to create a feeling of warmth and compassion for Future You. Think about a close friend you haven't seen in a long time, whom you miss and admire. Imagine that you're going to be seeing them soon and can't wait to see what they've accomplished with their life. You know they're up to something great, and you know you're going to be proud of them. And know that, as you move through your life with the generosity and compassion of mindfulness fueling your healthy caring adult, you are that person already.

As you continue on this journey of creatively being you, I'm grateful that you took me with you for some of the trip and that you worked with the ideas in this book to get to the root of coping patterns that may not have served you and tap in to a healthy, caring adult self who can serve you. If it turns out some of the skills and exercises in this book help you, I will be deeply humbled and happy to be a part of the process.

Acknowledgments

This book would not have been possible, first and foremost, without my clients, past and present, who have taught me so much, challenged me, and helped me grow as a caring human being.

Of course, I would never have been the person who could complete this project without the loving support, inspiration, joy, and pragmatism of my wife, Cathy. As ever.

My close friends offer ongoing support with everything. My deepest gratitude and affection go to Steven Reisner, Josh Berman, and Robert Devens. And special thanks to Richard Lasky, a great supervisor and all-around mensch.

Wendy Behary, who trained me as a schema therapist, has been steadfast and utterly reliable in her support for my growth as a schema therapist. Wendy is a wonderful role model for the spirit of schema therapy.

I will always hold affection for my colleagues in Wendy's original certification program in schema therapy: the Magnificent 12! Your kind group spirit was really my inspiration for me to continue with schema therapy.

I'd also like to warmly thank my supervisors, supporters, and clinical guides on my path, including Kathy Rudlin, John Gasiewski, Marsha Blank, Eckhard Roediger, Scott Kellogg, Evangelia Anthis, Peregrine Kavros, Tena Davies, and Susan Simpson. Warm thanks to Magdalena Kitlowska, my schema therapy "partner in crime."

I owe much gratitude to the entire membership community of the International Society of Schema Therapy, who have always been warm, supportive, and active. During my time on the Executive Board of the ISST, I deeply valued the comradery of my fellow board members, in particular Jeff Conway, whose warmth and humanity showed the way. And of course, I'd like to thank Jeffrey Young, for making schema therapy happen, and offering his generous support.

And finally, my deep gratitude to New Harbinger Publications and my editors, Jennye Garibaldi, Vicraj Gill, and Gretel Hakanson for their patience, hard work, wise guidance, and for believing in this project.

Appendix

I adapted exercises in this book from various works and schools of schema therapy. Particular attributions are listed below. And of course, the broad frameworks of schema therapy are drawn from the pioneering work of Jeffrey Young and Janet Klosko (1993) in their book *Reinventing Your Life* and of Jeffery Young, Janet Klosko, and Marjorie Weishaar (2003) in their book *Schema Therapy: A Practitioner's Guide.*

I would also like to highlight that this book is the result of my individual clinical experience as a schema therapist. I have made some adjustments in terminology in order to describe schema therapy concepts more clearly—for a popular audience. So some of my mode and schema terms will appear somewhat different from the theoretical texts geared toward practitioners listed below. Throughout this work, though, I endeavor to respect the core theory and fundamentals.

Chapter 2

- The discussion of core emotional needs is based on Jeffery Young, Janet Klosko, and Marjorie Weishaar's (2003) discussion in *Schema Therapy: A Practitioner's Guide* (9–10).

- The approach of focusing on "Little You" and work with photos comes from schema therapy training with Wendy Behary and The Cognitive Therapy Center of New Jersey and The Schema Therapy Institutes of NJ-NYC-DC.

Chapter 3

- The three priority schemas exercise employs the expressive writing technique as formulated by James Pennebaker and Joshua Smyth (Pennebaker and Smyth 2016).

Chapter 4

- The exercise "Identifying Your Modes" was certainly inspired by Eckhard Roediger, who uses a similar approach to visualizing modes in the consulting room. Roediger's work also inspired the "Theater of the Personality" exercise (Roediger et al. 2018, 41).

Chapter 5

- "Healthy Caring Adult Values" was also inspired by Eckhard Roediger (Roediger et al. 2018, 138–140). While my work on values in this chapter is based on my own clinical work, I remain indebted to their book for explicitly highlighting values in the experience of the healthy caring adult mode.

- "Healthy Caring Adult Journal" is based on the "therapy notebook" suggestion made by William Kuyken, Christine Padesky, and Robert Dudley (2009) for a client to use in therapy to document their strengths (103).

- "Six Principles of the Healthy Caring Adult" was inspired by Laurence Steinberg's (2004) *The 10 Basic Principles of Good Parenting.*

Chapter 6

- The "Mode Dialogue Practice" is inspired by the pioneering influence of Scott Kellogg (2015) on the technique of chair work (94–112).

- Eckhard Roediger, Bruce Stevens, and Robert Brockman (2018) bring innovation to the mode dialogue technique which influenced this section (179–197).

- Wendy Behary (2013) refers to the voice recording technique throughout her book.

- Jeffery Young, Janet Klosko, and Marjorie Weishaar (2003) use the term "mode dialogues" to describe chair work with modes (298–302).

- The six principles of managing modes with dialogue employ the concepts of limited reparenting and empathic confrontation as laid out by Jeffery Young, Janet Klosko, and Marjorie Weishaar (2003, 92–94, 182–186).

Chapter 7

- The "Guided Meditation for Modes" was influenced by:

  - a blend of techniques practiced by Thich Nhat Hanh and his followers in the Plum Village tradition as available on the Plum Village app, as well as documented in *Reconciliation: Healing the Inner Child* (Nhat Hanh 2010).

  - elements of "Mindfulness Daily" with Tara Brach and Jack Kornfield, as accessed online https://courses.tarabrach.com /courses/mindfulness-daily.

References

Behary, W. 2013. *Disarming the Narcissist*. Oakland, CA: New Harbinger Publications.

Behary, W. 2019. Personal communication. 2019 International Training and Certification Program in Schema Therapy. March 1–5. The Cognitive Therapy Center of New Jersey.

Hackmann, A., J. Bennett-Levy, and E. Holmes. 2011. *Oxford Guide to Imagery in Cognitive Therapy*. Oxford, UK: Oxford University Press.

Kellogg, S. 2015. *Transformational Chairwork*. Lanham, MD: Rowman and Littlefield.

Kuyken, W., C. A. Padesky, and R. Dudley. 2009. *Collaborative Case Conceptualization*. New York: The Guilford Press.

Nhat Hanh, Thich. 2010. *Reconciliation: Healing the Inner Child*. Berkeley, CA: Parallax Press.

Pennebaker, J. W., and J. M. Smyth. 2016. *Opening Up by Writing It Down*.
New York: The Guilford Press.

Roediger, E., B. Stevens, and R. Brockman. 2018. *Contextual Schema Therapy*. Oakland, CA: Context Press.

Steinberg, L. 2004. *The 10 Basic Principles of Good Parenting*. New York: Simon and Schuster.

Young, J. E., and J. S. Klosko. 1993. *Reinventing Your Life*. New York: Plume Penguin Group.

Young, J., J. Klosko, and M. Weishaar. 2003. *Schema Therapy A Practitioner's Guide*. New York: The Guilford Press.

Richard Brouillette, LCSW, is a certified schema therapist who works with entrepreneurs, creatives, and professionals seeking to overcome anxiety, find fulfillment, and improve their relationships. Brouillette has been published in *The New York Times* and *PsychCentral*, and is a *Psychology Today* expert opinion blogger. Brouillette is a former Secretary of the Executive Board of the International Society for Schema Therapy.

Foreword writer **Wendy T. Behary, LCSW**, is founder and clinical director of The Cognitive Therapy Center of New Jersey, founding fellow of the Academy of Cognitive Therapy, and author *Disarming the Narcissist*.

Real change *is* possible

For more than forty-five years, New Harbinger has published proven-effective self-help books and pioneering workbooks to help readers of all ages and backgrounds improve mental health and well-being, and achieve lasting personal growth. In addition, our spirituality books offer profound guidance for deepening awareness and cultivating healing, self-discovery, and fulfillment.

Founded by psychologist Matthew McKay and Patrick Fanning, New Harbinger is proud to be an independent, employee-owned company. Our books reflect our core values of integrity, innovation, commitment, sustainability, compassion, and trust. Written by leaders in the field and recommended by therapists worldwide, New Harbinger books are practical, accessible, and provide real tools for real change.

newharbingerpublications

MORE BOOKS from
NEW HARBINGER PUBLICATIONS

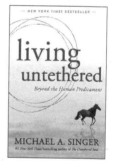

Did you know there are **free tools** you can download for this book?

Free tools are things like **worksheets, guided meditation exercises**, and **more** that will help you get the most out of your book.

You can download free tools for this book— whether you bought or borrowed it, in any format, from any source—from the New Harbinger website. All you need is a NewHarbinger.com account. Just use the URL provided in this book to view the free tools that are available for it. Then, click on the "download" button for the free tool you want, and follow the prompts that appear to log in to your NewHarbinger.com account and download the material.

You can also save the free tools for this book to your **Free Tools Library** so you can access them again anytime, just by logging in to your account! Just look for this button on the book's free tools page. ➤

+ Save this to my free tools library

If you need help accessing or downloading free tools, visit **newharbinger.com/faq** or contact us at **customerservice@newharbinger.com**.